IF
ONLY
YOU
WOULD
Change

IF ONLY YOU WOULD *Change*

MARK J. LUCIANO, PH. D.
& CHRISTOPHER MERRIS

Publishers Since 1798

THOMAS NELSON PUBLISHERS
NASHVILLE

Published in Nashville, Tennessee, by Thomas Nelson, Inc., and distributed in Canada by Lawson Falle, Ltd., Cambridge, Ontario.

Scripture quotations are from the NEW KING JAMES VERSION of the Bible. Copyright © 1979, 1980, 1982, Thomas Nelson, Inc., Publishers.

Although they are based on real cases and individuals, the characters and case studies described in this book are composites of several individuals and cases and are not intended to portray actual people.

Library of Congress Cataloging-in-Publication Data

Luciano, Mark J. (Mark Joseph)
    If only you would change / Mark J. Luciano & Christopher Merris.
      p.   cm.
    ISBN 0-8407-3423-9 (pb)
    1. Marriage. 2. Communication in marriage. 3. Twelve-step
programs. 4. Interpersonal relations. I. Merris, Christopher.
II. Title.
HQ734.L768   1992
646.7'8—dc20   91-44329
                                        CIP

Printed in the United States of America
1 2 3 4 5 6 7 — 97 96 95 94 93 92

*To Shelley, "the therapist's therapist,"
and to our children, Claire and Alexander*

*To each person who has come to us for help
with marriage problems and now is lovingly
on the road to recovery—this book is for you.*

The authors acknowledge their debt of gratitude to those who have stood by them with inspiration and encouragement, especially Linda Chester and Betty Youngs for taking us seriously; Roy M. Carlisle, Hank Stine, and Candice Fuhrman for their expertise, wit, and wisdom; Jane S. Jones, Ronald H. Haynes, and all the people at Thomas Nelson who have been so helpful. Finally, a special thanks to Donald C. Brandenburgh who made it all happen.

CONTENTS

The Twelve Steps   *viii*

Preface   *xi*

Introduction   *xiv*

1. Admission   *1*
2. Belief   *23*
3. Surrender   *40*
4. Moral Inventory   *51*
5. Confession   *81*
6. Readiness   *100*
7. Humility   *122*
8. Willingness   *139*
9. Making Amends   *161*
10. Perseverance   *182*
11. Contact   *198*
12. Recovery   *215*
    Notes   *225*
    Appendix   *227*

The Twelve Steps
of Alcoholics Anonymous*

1. We admitted we were powerless over alcohol—that our lives had become unmanageable.

2. Came to believe that a Power greater than ourselves could restore us to sanity.

3. Made a decision to turn our will and our lives over to the care of God as we understood Him.

4. Made a searching and fearless moral inventory of ourselves.

5. Admitted to God, to ourselves and to another human being the exact nature of our wrongs.

6. Were entirely ready to have God remove all these defects of character.

7. Humbly asked Him to remove our shortcomings.

8. Made a list of all persons we had harmed, and became willing to make amends to them all.

9. Made direct amends to such people wherever possible, except when to do so would injure them or others.

10. Continued to take personal inventory and when we were wrong promptly admitted it.

11. Sought through prayer and meditation to improve our conscious contact with God, as we understood Him, praying only for knowledge of His will for us and the power to carry that out.

12. Having had a spititual awakening as the result of these steps, we tried to carry this message to alcoholics, and to practice these principles in all our affairs.

---

*The Twelve Steps are reprinted and adapted with permission of Alcoholics Anonymous World Services, Inc. Permission to reprint the Twelve Steps does not mean that AA has reviewed or approved the content of this publication, nor that AA agrees with the views expressed herein. AA is a program of recovery from alcoholism. Use of the Twelve Steps in connection with programs and activities which are patterned after AA but which address other problems does not imply otherwise.

Twelve Steps
Adapted to Troubled Couples
Anonymous

1. We admitted we were powerless to change our spouses, that our marriage problems had become unmanageable.

2. We came to believe that a Power greater than ourselves could restore us to sanity.

3. We made a decision to turn our will and our lives over to the care of God, as we understood Him.

4. We made a searching and fearless moral inventory of ourselves.

5. Admitted to God, to ourselves, and to another human being the exact nature of our wrongs.

6. We were entirely ready to have God remove these defects of character.

7. We humbly asked God to remove our shortcomings.

8. Made a list of all persons we had harmed and became willing to make amends to them all.

9. Made direct amends to such people wherever possible, except when to do so would injure them or others.

10. We continued to take personal inventory and when we were wrong, promptly admitted it.

11. We sought through prayer and meditation to improve our conscious contact with God, as we understood Him, praying only for the knowledge of His will and the power to carry that out.

12. Having had a spiritual awakening as the result of these steps, we tried to carry this message to those in troubled marriage relationships, and to practice these principles in all our affairs.

PREFACE

When friends or relatives have marital difficulties, it places their friends and family members in the hopeless middle position of trying to help without interfering. You don't want to take sides or judge another person's choices, and yet it's hard to stand back and watch lives be torn apart.

It isn't any easier as a helping professional. Presumably people come to us for help. We try to understand but it's easy to get caught. If we side with the one partner, the other one gets upset and doesn't come back. If we don't agree, the first person doesn't return. Sometimes one partner will want to seek counseling and the other one won't participate in order to assert control. Sometimes the seeker of help is just looking for reinforcements to back up his or her own position. More than one couple has come to us with mouths agape saying, "The first counselor told us to get a divorce!" It is as though something else has to happen before effective counseling takes place, a preparation phase. As Carl Whitacker put it, "helping doesn't help." Whether you are a friend, relative, or professional, a person has to get ready to hear what you have to say before he or she will hear you.

Like most people do when faced with frustration, we looked around to see what everybody else was doing to help troubled couples. Professionally sponsored programs are great if you can convince people to go to them. At other times cost is a deterrent. Church based or community based programs are often stymied by the reluctance of poeple to openly acknowledge to their neighbors they are having marital problems. The only ones who didn't seem to be having any of these problems were the Twelve Step groups. So we started looking there.

During the holiday season of 1985, we began a group called "Holiday Helper" for individuals struggling with the holiday blues. Whether it was a troubled marriage, a temperamental teenager, or some other family struggle, everyone was welcome and we helped one another get through the holidays. We presented the Twelve Steps as our format and went from there. We soon saw what the folks at AA had been telling us. The Twelve Steps are a program for life.

For most of the people it was not that they had lots of problems. It was just that in one or two areas of their lives they had no control and that was disrupting everything. Counseling did not help, praying did not help. Nothing, it seemed had an effect. Until, of course, they started integrating the principles found in the Twelve Steps. Once we human beings decide what the problem is and how it ought to be fixed, most of us just keep on trying to solve the problems in the same way, even if the solutions don't work. We latch on to our solutions like grabbing hold of the handrail on a sinking ship. And the faster it goes down, the tighter we hold on, because either we are completely convinced there is no other way or we don't know what else to do. The missing piece is the spiritual dimension: the readiness to let go and let God.

People don't have big troubles for bad reasons. We have big troubles for good reasons. When it comes to family and especially spouses, often we have simply come to the end of our resources. There's no energy left. We don't have the skills needed, and so we keep on doing the only thing we know how to do, even when we know it won't solve the problem. We will keep on making the same mistakes, because it is the only way we know how to respond. That is where God comes in. Faith is what you do when you don't know what else to do. Faith *in someone or something* is what you turn to when you have done your best and it isn't enough.

There are some moments in life when things are very clear and you know what you must do. The answers are easy. There are other times when things aren't so clear but you have to act anyway. Faith means letting go of what is certain—the ship is going down—for something else which is still to come. It calls out of us courage, as well as fear, creativity, forgiveness, and commitment, but most of all trust.

The spiritual or faith dimension is something that has been left out of many people's problem-solving schemes for a long time. This includes solving marital problems. The consequence is increased rigidity and eccentricity. We, the authors, coming from a Christian perspective, feel this spiritual awakening is a determining factor in people's abilities to heal their troubled relationships. For it is not just the ability to understand another that makes for healthy relationships, it is also the ability to accept and embrace another in his or her difference, his or her otherness. This can be done effectively only with a healthy look inward. We have discovered this not only in working out troubles in our own relationships, but in watching others recover as well.

It is a fundamental spiritual truth that what happens to the human spirit will also happen to society. They are of one piece. The spiritual awakening promised by these Twelve Steps, therefore, invites us to believe in a new day for ourselves, every marriage and family, and our world.

Christopher Merris
Mark J. Luciano

INTRODUCTION

Never before in human history has change come so rapidly as it does in the times we live in. Relationships are changing dramatically in every sector of human life. The pressures brought to bear on partners in a marriage stem from within themselves as well as from without. They have to contend with influences they are responsible for—like their own personalities—as well as those that invade them from across the street, across generations, and from God knows where else! The struggle in a relationship, then, is not whether to change, but how to go through change and which changes will nurture the marriage as well as the partners in the marriage.

This dynamic setting makes it necessary to examine marital problems in an equally dynamic way. Couples experiencing strain in their marriages are inclined to feel the sting of resentment first and ask questions later. Each partner holds the other responsible for 100 percent of their behavior, but when it comes to his or her *own* actions, there are special circumstances. Let's face it, we all have reasons for doing what we do, and from our own perspective the reasons make our actions legitimate. But the consequences of those actions in the context of a relationship may have explosive results. So, even though we may be "right" in our actions on one level, the outcome may be disastrous.

Each of us lives in a web of relationships that is continuously affecting us. Job stress, strain coming from in-laws, neighborhood violence, to name a few, push the buttons of fear and anger as much as the individual behaviors of a marriage partner. You have to ask not just what are the problems with your marriage, but *why* are they a problem? Why do they cause you upset? Why are they upsetting you *now?* Are these troubles new or did you know about them when you got married? How are these troubles in your marriage related to other troubles in your life?

Change is never an easy thing. Even good changes like a new job or buying a new house provoke stress and anxiety. In writing this book, we have come to have a profound admiration for the men and women who undertake marriage. Married couples say to each other, "Not only do we have a loving relationship now, but as we go through the changes of life, our relationship will be the common thread, the common theme that runs throughout."

History testifies to humanity's adaptability. The human mind is versatile, creative, courageous, persistent. Especially in times of trouble, inventiveness and perseverance have emerged to guide individuals and couples to new solutions, new relationships. The Twelve Steps made famous by Alcoholics Anonymous are a profoundly reliable way to undergo change in one's life. Born from the nightmare of alcoholism, these twelve steps have been a guiding light for millions of people in seemingly hopeless situations.

In fact, since their publication in 1934, the Twelve Steps have helped millions of alcoholics, drug abusers, gamblers, child abusers, sex addicts, and chronic victims to turn their lives around and become productive, self-fulfilled individuals. Encouraged by this, people who found themselves wrestling with other kinds of addictive or obsessive behaviors adapted the Twelve Step program to their own needs and were able, once again, to break the cycle, stop destructive behaviors, and maintain recovery from them.

Eventually it was discovered that all addictive/obsessive behaviors affect the spouse and children of the addict. Because the family functions as a unit, the disease of one member creates a relationship of codependency in which the family members exhibit symptoms of dysfunction—and here, too, the Twelve Step programs were effective in helping end the cycle and in promoting new, healthier behavior.

The culprit that alienates couples and disables their adaptive skills is *resentment*. Resentment breaks down trust and intimacy. Resentment leads partners in troubled marriages to the irrational conviction that *if only my partner would change this character defect, the marriage would be perfect.* There are certainly many troubling issues affecting marriage, such as affairs, abuse, sexual dysfunction. But what stifles change and sabotages the healing process is resentment, the desire to extract some payment from your partner for hurt you believe he or she has caused you.

The question, then, is not the fact of change in your relationship, but what changes are needed and how skillfully can you go through them? Furthermore, it is not simply a matter of staying married. Many couples will maintain a relatively stable yet unhealthy marriage. They will hold the marriage together at all costs. Those costs may be an anorexic child, physical and emotional abuse, a psychosomatic ailment, or just chronic unhappiness. What is needed for individuals in a troubled marriage is a way to openly and honestly examine the true nature of the relationship and, in an equally honest and open way, discern the best direction for the marriage. The principles contained in this volume teach you to direct your emotional, physical, and spiritual energy away from obsessively trying to change your partner in order to fulfill your own needs, thereby freeing your partner to make similar choices.

The Twelve Steps form the outline for your progress. They have been tried and found to be effective in a variety of situations. Anyone who sincerely works through these steps will experience a change within themselves, and consequently, the nature of their relationships will change too. All you need is to ask someone who is following this path of recovery, and they will be more than happy to explain how it has helped them.

Just as the Twelve Steps chart a specific path, the addition of certain techniques of cognitive therapy provides excellent help for integrating the principles of the Twelve Steps. We all have skills we use for adapting to changing circumstances. These strategies work up to a point. They are appropriate within certain parameters and for certain durations of time. Beyond these boundaries our way of handling various kinds of conflicts, discussing sensitive topics, or living with certain kinds of pressure may need to be modified. If problems are not being resolved, the difficulty may lie not with the problem but with the solutions. The Step Guides given in this book are designed to help you frame the problem and the solution in a constructive way so as to make progress.

The Twelve Steps can be used in conjunction with other therapy programs you are currently working. In fact, for some marital difficulties professional counseling is necessary. A self-help program for improving your marriage is not like tinkering on the family car. Solutions are sometimes more complex than home remedies can provide.

You will find the steps follow each other logically. But most people find they frequently need to go back to preceding steps. Once you have completed Step One, for example, the work of implementing Step Four may expose areas over which you are not completely convinced you are powerless. The wisdom of the steps builds with each step you take. Likewise, it will be clear that no step can be skipped successfully. There are no magic secrets exposed in this volume. In fact, we have tried to present the ideas in as simple a fashion as possible. Each marriage is unique. Each person has his or her own particular circumstances and journey. The ideas in this book are meant to strengthen what is truly unique about each individual and to free them up so as to be able to freely choose and act in a loving, honest, and just way. The best success comes from patiently persevering one day at a time.

When working through the steps we recommend keeping a journal. The process of thinking through a problem and writing down your thoughts, no matter how jumbled, helps to increase your awareness of not only what is going on around you, but within you. As you will soon see, it is not just troubles between you and your spouse that you will be discussing, but also the state of being within yourself. The harmony you possess within your own heart will spill over into your marriage. Keeping a journal helps nurture the spirit within you.

Another important element in the program is the use of a sponsor. A sponsor is someone who has also chosen to follow the Twelve Steps to recover lost sobriety or serenity in his or her life. Sponsors are an irreplaceable source of wisdom that cannot be obtained from a book. Sometimes it takes another flesh-and-blood person to be a companion on the road to recovery.

Twelve Step meetings are another vital link with the power of this program. Troubled Couples Anonymous groups are being formed nationally and can be started by any two or more people who choose to work these steps and follow the Twelve Step traditions. These group meetings can take a variety of shapes. They may include sharing sessions, speaker meetings, or step studies. Since this is a program for individuals in troubled marriages, it is not necessary or even advisable for couples to go to the same meeting. The anonymity of your partner should be maintained as well as your own.

Finally there have been many individuals we have encountered during the course of our work that have exhibited remarkable courage and wisdom in the way they have nurtured their marriages. Though it seems only the horror stories are publicized, there are many more untold stories of genuine faith and devotion. If you are in a troubled marriage now, be of good cheer. You won't be for long. Even the couples who, after working through these steps, decided to go their separate ways did so for all the right reasons, rather than out of hatred or self-destructive impulses. They ended something that needed to be ended and began a new chapter of their lives on a happy, healthy footing.

There are many who have gone before you in seeking to renew their lives by means of these Twelve Steps. Their stories are grateful testimonies to the effectiveness of the Twelve Steps. Your journey will be unique, as you are unique. But as you work your program you will never be alone in the struggles and setbacks. There is a fellowship of others who will be walking with you.

1

ADMISSION

STEP ONE: WE ADMITTED WE WERE POWERLESS TO CHANGE OUR SPOUSES, THAT OUR MARRIAGE PROBLEMS HAD BECOME UNMANAGEABLE.

For twenty-five years Laura had been the faithful wife. Bob was a good man but admittedly not the easiest person to live with. He was hot tempered and stubborn. Nonetheless, Laura, a woman of strong moral conviction, was determined to make her marriage work. Then one day she discovered that not only was Bob having an affair, but that it probably was not the first.

Paula has been through a lot with Greg. He is a recovering alcoholic with three years' sobriety. But even though he has stopped drinking, there are still problems in their marriage. Greg is a successful businessman and an excellent provider for his family. However, Paula feels she is treated like a child because she must always ask him for money and give an account for every dollar she spends. Greg has a tendency to lecture Paula rather than listen to her when she needs his support.

Phil and Joanne are in a "cold war." Over the ten years of their marriage they have grown emotionally distant, choosing more and more to lead separate lives. Joanne has become rigid and irritable about almost everything, from

1

her kitchen and laundry room to their social plans. Though dissatisfied with his marriage, Phil lacks the courage to break through the ice.

Laura, Paula, and Phil have something very important in common: Each has persistent marriage problems. Each knows exactly which characteristics of his or her partner must change if these marriage problems are ever to improve. Each has tried several strategies to improve the relationship, but simply asking for change from their spouses has not worked.

Each time Laura confronts Bob about his infidelity, he goes into a rage. She manages to tell Bob she will not tolerate another affair, but finds it impossible to discuss the issue with him further because of his blowups. Whenever Paula asks Greg for more emotional support, she receives a lecture on how to avoid becoming so upset over trivia. Long ago Phil stopped trying to confront Joanne about her rigidity. At the very mention of it she becomes sullen, withdrawn, and irritable.

Laura, Paula, and Phil resent their partners' reactions. They are at their wits' ends because nothing they have tried has worked. "If only you would change," they say, "we could be happy."

OBSESSION: THE ADDICTION OF THE PARTNER IN A TROUBLED MARRIAGE

A problem becomes an obsession when it dominates your life. You think about the problem constantly. It colors your perception of everything and everyone. Your whole frame of reference is focused on the troublesome issue.

Laura became obsessed about Bob and their marriage problems. She was depressed almost all the time. She could not sleep. She overate. Her concentration at work was poor. Her thoughts were confused. At one moment she was angry at Bob, accusing him of throwing twenty-five years of her life out the window. The next moment she would turn the anger inward, berating herself for being overweight and unattractive to him.

Thoughts about the future went around and around in her head. How could she trust him again? Would she leave him?

Laura shared her story with the other members of her Twelve Step group. "Bob and I have been through so much," she said. "We've raised three children. It's hard to think that we may not stay together. I always suspected Bob slept with other women, but I could never prove it. Part of his role in our business is to drive a transport truck and sometimes he has to stay overnight in L.A. When I found a woman's lipstick in the truck I knew for sure.

"When I confronted him about it, he didn't even try to deny it. He just said, as cold as ice, 'That's the way I am.' I told him I would leave him if it continued and he just grunted that it wouldn't. I don't want to leave. All my friends have told me that I'm a fool for staying with him, but we have so much invested in each other. If only Bob would stop his affairs and control his temper, everything would be fine. We get along in every other area. I know that if he doesn't change in these two areas, we just aren't going to make it."

THE OBJECT OF OBSESSION: YOUR SPOUSE'S CHARACTER DEFECT

Paula stayed with Greg through the difficult years of his alcoholic drinking. Since his recovery three years ago, she works the Al-Anon Twelve Step program as Greg attends Alcoholics Anonymous. Paula works at letting go of the resentment she holds toward Greg for all the years he drank. The most hurtful effect of Greg's drinking was his tendency to pick a fight and then "turn the tables," making it appear that everything was Paula's fault.

"Greg would go out and drink all night. He wouldn't even call to tell me where he was. I'd wonder if he were alive or dead, if he'd been in a drunk-driving accident. Then the next day not a word would pass between us until he found something to attack me for. One time it was the refrigerator. It was cluttered and messy and therefore I was a bad wife. That upset me and I began to cry. But he's the one who was out drinking all night!"

When Greg achieved sobriety, their life together changed dramatically, but their problems were not over. "Now Greg doesn't drink. He doesn't pick stupid fights to shift the blame to me anymore. I forgive him for all the times that he did because he doesn't do it anymore, and I know he regrets the way he mistreated me. The only thing is that when we do fight, it still appears that everything—whatever it is we're fighting about—is my fault again!

"Greg has always been a great provider financially for the family. He's been completely responsible for the money. That's one of the things we fight about most. But it's not really about money. It's about control. We finally agreed that I would have my own account and my own money, but Greg keeps reasserting control in little ways.

"Like when I wanted to open an arts and crafts business at the swap meet. I had to invest a small amount of money to get it started. Greg was so negative about it! I know he tried to restrain himself. It just would have been nice if he could have been supportive instead of critical. Being a businessman I'm sure he saw a dozen problems with the idea. I wouldn't mind constructive input at all, but negative, critical input I can do without."

Paula thought Greg was analytical and critical toward her. This got to her. "Greg can be so generous and giving. As part of his recovery he stepped up his volunteer time on community projects and added time working in Alcoholics Anonymous. He can be generous, positive, and supportive with just about everyone except me.

"Everything else about Greg is wonderful! If only he could change this one thing about his personality, everything would be okay. . . ."

THE OBSESSION AND THE DOWNWARD SPIRAL

Phil is very discouraged about his marriage. He does not see how he and his wife, Joanne, can come out of the emotional slump they have fallen into. He has become obsessed with her character defects. He doubts whether a Twelve Step program or any counseling will get them out of the ten-year rut they are in.

"There is a kind of Pandora's box of issues that you just can't discuss with Joanne. They make her mad and then it's all over. I don't feel like I can talk to her."

Phil and Joanne are in a "cold war." There are no open arguments or fighting. To keep peace Phil avoids any issues that disturb her. He knows some of these issues are unimportant, like the fact that Joanne wants her kitchen kept a certain way and will get mad if he doesn't put things away right. But Phil is not always sure what the right way is, and because she becomes so annoyed with him about it, he has stopped using the kitchen.

Then there is the laundry. Phil tried to help out by doing an occasional load, but Joanne complained he never did it right. He stopped doing that too.

Phil is anxious about doing anything around the house. His only exclusive domain, it seems, is the backyard and the garage. He feels like the house is Joanne's territory and outside is his. That makes him mad.

"Don't I pay for most of this? Why is it that I feel like a stranger in my own house?" Phil never says what is really on his mind, because he knows Joanne will get upset.

Joanne has long since given up trying to explain to Phil what annoys her. From her point of view, he never really listens to her anyway. Part of the trouble, she thinks, is Phil's age. Now in his early sixties, Phil is more than ten years older than Joanne. He sometimes has trouble remembering what Joanne tells him to do.

The most important part of the problem is that Phil has "shut down." He has stopped trying to explain to Joanne what upsets him. They have learned to "live around" one another and not get in each other's way. Naturally, this is not fulfilling to either of them. Anger and frustration build inside them both, and though they know they are not happy, neither feels confident to make the first move. They are unwilling to take the risk.

An uneasy peace has developed over the years. The frustration Phil and Joanne feel about their marriage came to a peak, however, when their youngest child was about to leave home. They both knew something had to be done, because soon there would be no one home but the two of them. The chill in their relationship would have to end.

Each of these three couples illustrates in their own unique ways the remarkably similar development of entrenched and apparently unsolvable marriage problems. These are not marriage problems that respond to a short course of marriage counseling, communication skills training, or the like. They are, rather, the result of "normal" marriage problems made worse and seemingly unresolvable by the obsession with a spouse's character defects and the resentment that develops over them.

Have you said something similar about your own marriage? Have you felt that if your partner would change just one or two things about himself or herself the marriage would be fine? When you sort through the various issues affecting your marriage, doesn't it actually come down to one or two fundamental complaints? Check your marriage against the items on the Marital Needs Inventory and identify those that best describe what you think are key problems.

MARITAL NEEDS INVENTORY

1. My spouse does not spend enough time talking with me about feelings, the day's events, and so forth.

2. One of us is often dissatisfied with the degree of emotional intimacy and affection in our relationship.

3. My spouse berates, criticizes, or "tears down" me or my side of the family.

4. Slight disagreements seem to turn into crises with us.

5. My spouse simply does not measure up to my expectations in some areas.

6. My spouse has never really achieved what he or she is truly capable of.

7. One of us does not feel he or she understands what the other is upset about.

8. Problems in our marriage seem to linger without progress toward a solution.

9. One of us feels that he or she must always give in to the other.

10. We often lapse into an argument or fight even when we begin discussing a problem calmly.

11. One of us feels that the other spends too much money on some things or not enough on others.

12. There is basic disagreement on how we should spend/ invest money.

13. One of us feels limited by the marriage in the sense that the relationship stifles him or her as an individual.

14. One of us feels that the other holds him or her back from doing or achieving things that would make him or her a happier, more fulfilled person.

15. One of us feels that the other does not pull his or her own weight in terms of household chores or work outside the home.

16. One of us feels that the other is not completely honest with the other.

17. One of us wants to make love more frequently than the other.

18. One of us is continually dissatisfied with the quality of lovemaking.

19. One of us is much more strict in parenting than the other.

20. My spouse and I disagree on what the children should be taught in terms of morality (i.e., right and wrong/good and evil).

21. My spouse drinks or uses drugs too much.

22. My spouse hits or physically hurts me or the children.

23. My spouse has had or continues to have extramarital sexual involvement.

24. My spouse is verbally and/or emotionally abusive to me or the children.

25. My spouse is degrading or abusive toward me in our sexual relationship.

NOTE: If you have marked *any* item 21–25, it is advised that you immediately seek professional help.

Later in the chapter we'll look at these questions in more detail, but for now, of the items you checked, which are the most hurtful and distressing? These items represent your unfulfilled needs—the needs you long for your spouse to fulfill. The hurt you feel as a result of these unfulfilled needs drives the obsession.

Obsession with your spouse's character defects moves in a declining spiral. The obsession begins when you first perceive your spouse's character defects. It accelerates when you allow the real and imagined injuries you've received to turn into resentment. It becomes an addictive cycle, destructive to your marriage, when resentment develops into a habit—that is, an addiction.

RESENTMENT

Marriage, naturally, teaches you a lot about your spouse. However, it is double-edged, for, not only do you see the traits you admire in your spouse, you witness his or her character flaws as well.

For a time you can live with these imperfections. You ignore them or excuse them. It may be many years before you even identify your spouse's character defects. Sooner or later though, they rise up and become completely distracting. So, you mention to your spouse that something is bothering you. It blows up in your face and you feel hurt.

This is an unavoidable moment in every long-standing relationship. It is the outgrowth of living and working together. It happens because you have so much of yourself at stake in the marriage. Your marriage is the principal relationship of your adult life. It is a major enterprise for bringing fulfillment to your life.

The first time you make yourself vulnerable and you get burned, a scar forms. It may or may not be a serious fight that causes it, but the damage is done. You learn to be cautious about opening yourself up again. And yet, that is what intimacy requires. When the fear of being hurt keeps you from entering into honest, sincere communication with your spouse, it is called *resentment*.

Resentment occurs whether hurts are intentional or accidental. Maybe your spouse's character defects are mere personality quirks; perhaps they are serious disorders. Resentment is not the only marriage problem, but it lies at the heart of every marriage problem. Resolving conflicts with your spouse is impossible without first dealing with the effects of your own resentment.

Step One calls for you to admit that you cannot manage your marriage problems by yourself. This means that you recognize the futility of your attempts to change your spouse and your powerlessness over his or her character defects. Resentment has made your marriage problems unmanageable. Your life and marriage have become more and more unsatisfactory because your human needs are not being met. It is, in fact, the effort to manage or control others that hastens the decline of intimacy.

THE SPIRITUAL PROCESS OF ADDICTION

The spiritual process of addiction[1] is the pattern of attitudes, beliefs, actions, and reactions that leads to an unhealthy dependence on something, such as a drug or a behavior. It is a process because it develops over time and involves the incorporation of many experiences, ideas, and people. It is a spiritual process because it involves your total being, your physical, emotional, and psychic strengths, and your vital energies—everything that comes to you and from within you. Every other relationship is subjugated to your relationship to the addiction. Addiction is not simply physical—although obviously that is affected. It affects the way you think, which affects the way you feel. Unlike genuine needs that you depend on for life, addictions are self-destructive. That is, the more you indulge in your addictions the more disruptive to your life they become.

In a troubled marriage the addiction is not to a substance or drug, nor is it to a compulsive behavior like gambling or eating. The addiction in a troubled marriage is an addiction specifically to a *way of thinking*. It is an obsession.

Resentment sabotages problem-solving strategies by misleading problem-solving capabilities. Reasoning powers are used to justify actions. Emotions are fearful and defensive. The will is paradoxically set against solving the very problem causing the pain. Instead of solving the problem, you look for revenge; you want to punish your partner. "It is plain that a life which includes deep resentment leads only to futility and unhappiness."[2]

The addiction to resentment develops as follows:

- A real or imagined injury is perpetrated against you by your spouse.

- You hold on to this injury by placing the wrong or infraction "on the books" against your spouse.

- The perceived wrong becomes the main focus, while your own role and responsibility are minimized. Your partner's wrong is in clear focus. Your own is only partly recognized.

- The incident(s) is remembered and played back in your mind. The resentment is reinforced.

- Self-justification results. You are in the right; your spouse is in the wrong. It feels good, therefore, to hold on to the resentment. It becomes a type of drug to ease the pain of the marriage conflict.

- The use of resentment increases and becomes a habit. As resentment increases, more thoughts of self-justification are necessary to justify the presence of so much resentment. Thus, the resentment feeds on itself, taking on a life of its own in a vicious cycle.

- There is pain associated with the resentment also. Part of you is aware that the use of long-held anger and resentment is unhealthy. However, your partner continues in his or her character defects and fuels the resentment further. You alternate between feeling guilty at times for holding the resentment and feeling fully justified at others in holding to the resentment. Emotional isolation from your spouse increases.

- You try to abstain from thoughts of resentment, because you know it is unhealthy. However, "withdrawal" pain sets in. When you begin to abstain from resentment you are no longer justified. Your spouse is no longer completely or even mostly wrong. You are not completely or mostly right. The reality of your own part in the conflict comes clear to you. Your partner acts out of his or her character defect once again, and you find yourself back into the obsession.

Resentment is any strong anger or deep sadness that is held against your spouse for something he or she did that hurt you. When a couple first marries, each ignores much of what is annoying about the other, such as eating habits or cleanliness. At some point, however, one has "had it" and lashes out at the other. The confrontation results in a "clearing of the air." They talk it over and come to some agreement. The issue is finished.

But the cycle of resentment builds when the issue is never confronted or if, after the argument is over, the pain of the confrontation causes one or the other to hold on to the pain and anger, to remember it. The individual formulates an internal message like, "I'm never going to try *that* again," or "I'm afraid to express myself." The memory of the confrontation blocks the resumption of the relationship. Reconciliation does not quite happen. The glamour fades from the relationship. There is caution instead of spontaneity. Bitterness develops within. Fear begins to place a barrier between the two partners.

In the cold war Phil and Joanne were battling, Phil avoided bringing up touchy issues because he knew that would set Joanne off. Instead of working through the "rules of the kitchen," the major bone of contention, Phil simply gave up using the kitchen. That was Joanne's territory and he would just stay out. Up front, it looked as though he had settled the issue, but of course he harbored his anger within. He had enjoyed puttering around the kitchen from which he was now cut off. But more importantly, he felt alienated from his wife.

OBSESSION AND CONTROL

At first glance, the preoccupation with your spouse's character defects appears well justified. He or she does drink too much, eat too much, is verbally abusive, and so on. Perhaps your spouse's character defect has to do with manners or the way he or she dresses. Perhaps your partner lacks ambition and the will to improve. However, as the preoccupation continues, your thoughts about your spouse's character defect become obsessive. You come up with explanations for why your spouse is the way he or she is.

According to Aaron Beck, "What forces the differences to escalate to serious conflict are the unpleasant explanations for the spouse's actions. These negative explanations often lead to hostility, which in turn generates a new set of even *more* negative meanings, until finally the other person is seen in a completely negative light as a 'bitch' or 'bully.' "[3] As these negative explanations become more firmly believed, your own faults become obscured. The main problem is always thought to lie in your partner's shortcomings. Yes, these shortcomings are real, but the obsessive focus on your partner distorts your perspective of your own role in the conflict. You cannot always see it, but your own character traits work in tandem with your spouse's. Therefore, your partner's character traits—for better or worse—must be recognized as triggering positive or negative traits in you.

In the case of Greg and Paula, Paula was using her resentment as leverage to try to get Greg to change. She wanted Greg to give her support, not criticism. The strength of her obsessiveness and resentment toward Greg, however, practically guaranteed he would not change. But Paula could not see this. From her point of view, Greg was more wrong than right. She was the victim of what alcoholics call *pride-blindness*. She was blind to her addiction. She believed Greg was the cause of her resentment. If she could not get Greg to change, at least she could get back at him by being angry with him. This did, after all, have a temporary effect on him. In this way Paula held on to her control over Greg.

The intermeshing of traits that creates this downward spiral in marriage is what is commonly called *codependency*. A simple definition of codependency is "the tendency to take the responsibilities of another as your own." In a troubled marriage, codependency is the tendency to take your spouse's responsibility to work on his or her character defect as your responsibility. Not only will codependency not cause your spouse to change, it will destroy your marriage.

OBSESSION AND NEEDS

Codependency displays itself in various kinds of controlling behavior aimed at getting those unfulfilled needs met. Nagging or sulking are two examples. Recall that Phil was obsessed with changing Joanne's rigidity and irritability. They began to live around each other, avoiding any possibility of conflict. This eliminated many of the fights, but left them lonely and ill at ease.

Phil needed warmth and intimacy in his marriage, a very legitimate need in every person. It went unfulfilled, though, because of the cold distance Joanne kept. A wall had built up between them. Because the wall built up over time, he no longer experienced the resentment as resentment. He simply responded philosophically thinking, "That's just the way it is."

Deep down inside he wanted things to be different. Yet he believed it could never be because Joanne would never change. This belief was the basis of his resentment and why he saw her as the one to blame for the problems in their marriage. He felt this resentment when Joanne showed impatience with him. He felt degraded, disrespected, and unappreciated.

HALTING THE DOWNWARD SPIRAL—TAKING STEP ONE

Each of these three couples appears to be on the horns of a dilemma. Phil needs intimacy with Joanne. Paula needs support from Greg. Laura needs respect from Bob. Since these needs are legitimate and their spouses seem unwilling to change, what can they do? It takes two to make a marriage work. If one is not willing to take part, can anything be done?

Yes! The answer lies not in changing your partner or your needs, but changing the way you go about getting your needs met. This is the work of the twelve steps outlined in this book. The road to recovery begins by taking Step One.

UNMANAGEABILITY

Step One calls for you to admit that you cannot manage your marriage problems by yourself. This means you recognize the ineffectiveness of your attempts to change your spouse's character defect. The marriage has become unmanageable. It is out of your control. The recognition of unmanageability extends to other people, places, and events. In fact, it is the effort to manage or control others that hastens the downward spiral. Halting the downward spiral and healing the marriage mean recognizing that things are truly out of your control.

POWERLESSNESS AND SURRENDER

Powerlessness is a concept that has broad implications for how you approach your marriage relationship. Your marriage is unmanageable because you are fundamentally powerless to control your spouse, his or her character defect, and many of the events that happen to you. In Step One you admit the strategies you have tried have not worked and that every attempt to change or control your spouse will fail.

Admitting you are powerless implies a surrender to or acceptance of this fact. Surrender does not sound like much of a solution. But surrender here means surrendering the obsession to try to change your spouse. It is this obsession that blocks your genuine intellectual, emotional, and spiritual power.

If you are powerless to change your spouse, what are you to do? Commit yourself to working a careful program of recovery, one day at a time. The obsessive searchlight trained on your spouse will be refocused to look at what is within your power to change, namely yourself. The energy spent worrying and fretting over what your spouse will do next is more effectively used to fulfill your own needs. As you implement each new step, you will find you have recovered more and more of your life's energy.

SERENITY

Serenity is a relative state of being that comes from acknowledging your powerlessness over people and events. It is more than a mood, because it can occur whether you are happy or sad. It is a spiritual awareness that your needs are being taken care of by a higher power. This does not mean everything is perfect. It does not mean there are no goals to strive for. Rather, it is a contentment with and acceptance of yourself and your marriage as it is today, if only for today.

What feeds the obsession to focus on your spouse is the belief that your own needs are not being met and your spouse is the cause of their not being met. Serenity comes by taking responsibility for your own needs yourself and not depending on your spouse or others to fulfill them. Serenity is analogous to sobriety in Alcoholics Anonymous. But abstinence is only the beginning. Just because an alcoholic is not drinking does not mean he or she has recovered and is happy. Just the removal of his or her obsession does not automatically solve the problem. Anyone who has tried to quit smoking or to diet knows all they can think about is having a smoke or something to eat. Serenity comes when you believe your needs will be met.

Demanding from your spouse what you need to derive from within yourself is the main hurdle overcome by acknowledging powerlessness. Instead of expecting your spouse to rescue you from your insecurities or make you feel good about yourself, discover the real goodness that is in you. Serenity, then, is the result of a spiritual awakening within you that gives you the power to fulfill your needs.

WHAT DO I DO FIRST?

The first thing to do to stop the downward spiral of your marriage is to surrender. Stop trying to have a perfect marriage by being a perfect wife or a perfect husband. Stop trying to "fix" your spouse so that he or she will be a perfect spouse. Stop using abusive behavior as a way of gaining control over your spouse and the other members of your family. Stop putting guilt trips on yourself for not being perfect in every way. Stop the affairs. You cannot tell yourself you will improve your marriage while you are still practicing old destructive habits.

Commit yourself to the marriage and to a program of recovery for at least one hundred days. This will give you time to look at yourself and counteract the distortion caused by your unmet needs and the destructive habits that resentment causes. Make this commitment by reciting an affirmation every morning, such as:

> I promise just for today to work my Twelve Step program to the best of my ability. I surrender my desire to be right and perfect in my marriage relationship. I release my spouse from the obligation to be perfect. In particular, just for today, I now accept the part of my spouse's character that I find most unacceptable. I resolve to concentrate on my own growth and my own needs through the tools available to me in my Twelve Step program.

Just saying you are going to stop something does not mean you will automatically stop the behavior. You have to follow it with action. Implementing the principles outlined in these twelve steps will give you the help you need. They are not theoretical steps, but practical actions you can take to improve yourself and your marriage.

Start by getting out of yourself. Go to meetings. Get involved in a Twelve Step group. Get to know the members. Find someone you can call when you are having a tough time. Early in your recovery it is important to establish contact with others who are working the program. Isolating yourself from others is a clear sign that you have controlling attitudes.

SPONSORS

One valuable aid to recovery is the help of a good sponsor. Sponsors are guides or friends who are also practicing the Twelve Step principles in their own lives. As soon as you have committed yourself to seriously following the program, you should find a sponsor.

The emotional and spiritual turmoil you go through is draining. The aid of someone who understands your situation will help you move along more quickly and help you avoid certain pitfalls. Your sponsor should have achieved a level of recovery in his or her own marriage and be ahead of you in implementing the Twelve Steps. Follow his or her direction and keep in regular contact. At least once a week you should have a face-to-face meeting. During the initial period of recovery, daily contact by telephone and/or more frequent meetings may be required. Generally men should choose male sponsors and women female sponsors. If you are working the program as a couple, another more experienced couple may sponsor you and your partner together.

Your sponsor does not need to be perfect. The sponsor will not have all the answers and must be willing to say so. But the message of the program is brought to you through your sponsor. Sponsors are not marriage counselors nor do they bear responsibility for the success or failure of your marriage. Moreover, a sponsor should maintain an independence, or detachment, from the individual being sponsored so that the person might make personal choices and bear responsibility for his or her own life. The relationship between the individual and the sponsor is confidential, but it is not exclusive.

The sponsor lends support to the common goal of recovery. As you discover the various reasons for unhappiness in your marriage, your sponsor encourages you each step of the way toward recovery. Your sponsor is your companion in this journey, and both of you gain from the relationship. Both are encouraged to continue working your individual programs.

STEP GUIDE: STEP ONE

PART ONE

You have already begun to take Step One by addressing the chief needs in your relationship. The items you marked on pages 6–8 reflect physical, spiritual, or psychological needs. Needs are not options. They are different from wants or wishes. Fulfilling your needs is necessary if you are to become healthy and fulfilled.

Write down the items from page 19 that you consider to be your partner's most distressing character defects. Include also others not mentioned in the Marital Needs Inventory. Write these in a journal or diary so you can keep track of your progress.

PART TWO

Looking over the items you marked on pages 6–8, find the item(s) most distressing to you on the Marital Needs Inventory Chart.

MARITAL NEEDS INVENTORY CHART[4]

ITEMS	CHARACTER DEFECTS	NEEDS	VIRTUES
1, 2	Indifference/Withdrawal	Affection	Intimacy/Tenderness
3, 4	Degradation/Abusiveness	Respect	Admiration/Esteem
5, 6	Inadequacy/Incompetency	Skill	Competency/Achievement
7, 8	Distortion/Insensitivity	Understanding	Empathy/Sensitivity
9, 10	Aggressiveness/Coercion	Power & Influence	Cooperation/Inspiration
11, 12	Wastefulness/Poverty	Economic Well-being	Productivity/Resourcefulness
13, 14	Anxiety/Irritability	Personal Well-being	Happiness/Satisfaction
15, 16	Selfishness/Infidelity	Responsibility	Authenticity/Commitment
17, 18	Self-absorption/Alienation	Sexual Fulfillment	Enjoyment/Integration
19, 20	Abusiveness/Ineffectiveness	Parenting	Nurturance/Effectiveness
21, 22, 23, 24, 25*	*21–25 If you have marked any of these items, it is advised that you immediately seek professional help.		

From the chart you can see that for each character defect you identified in your spouse there is a corresponding need in you that is left unfulfilled. In the third column is the character strength or virtue your spouse will need to exercise for your need to be met.

PART THREE

1. Write down which of your spouse's character defects most distresses you.

2. Write a brief account of the first time this character defect became an issue with you and your spouse. If you cannot remember the first time, pick an incident early in the relationship that illustrates the conflict. Next answer the following questions:

How did you feel toward your (future) spouse regarding this issue? List the feelings and rate their intensity from one to one hundred.

How did you perceive yourself in the relationship? Did you feel dependent on your partner? Did you feel in control of the situation?

Did you minimize the importance of the conflict afterward? Did you "awfulize" the conflict (perceive it as much worse than it really was)?

How did you respond to the issue? Were you silent? Was there a fight? Did you blame your spouse? If you did, for what in particular?

What steps, if any, did you take to resolve the conflict? How effective were they? How did your partner react to your effort to resolve the conflict?

3. Now that you have examined the first incident in which your spouse's character defect became a serious issue in your relationship, recall other major incidents that reflect the development of the conflict over this character defect. As you recall these events, develop a chronology of each incident.

4. You now have an account of the first major conflict with your spouse, a reflection on that conflict, and a list of subsequent incidents. Next, take each major incident, an incident when you thought this character defect became worse, and reflect on your perceptions of it. Recall your feelings at the time.

5. Take inventory of the effect your partner's character defect has had on you by answering the following questions:

Growing intolerance: When your efforts to change your spouse's behavior failed, how did you react? Did it take more energy to function normally? Did you have to "psyche" yourself in order to get through a family meal? Did relatives and friends notice tension between you and your spouse? What were the ways you tried to cover up the problems?

Growing alienation: Did you try to avoid quiet moments alone with your spouse? Were you uneasy with attempts by your spouse to show affection? Did you mechanically go through the motions or hurry through them?

Growing preoccupation: Did you rearrange your lifestyle in order to avoid conflicts? Did you work longer hours or different shifts? Did you get involved in charitable work or other community activities to avoid being at home or to cover over loneliness?

Growing emotional distress: Did you become depressed or experience weight gain or loss? Did you have trouble sleeping or begin sleeping longer hours? Have you had crying spells? Did you feel angry and discontent most of the time?

Children: If you have children, how has the marital discord affected your relationship with them? Did you ever bargain for their affection or try to sabotage your spouse's relationship with them?

Home remedies: How did you try to "quick-fix" the marriage on your own? Did you try talking it out? Did you make agreements with each other that were never kept? Did you have a family member or friend try to mediate? Did you try to dramatize your point (for example, trying to "turn the tables" so that he or she would "know what it feels like")?

Loss of control: At a certain point it was not the problems between you that caused the difficulties, it was the obsession to change your spouse who became "the enemy." How has your life become unmanageable in the following areas?

Social: Did you lose friends, discontinue hobbies or community activities, or attend fewer social gatherings with your spouse? Have you felt embarrassed by the tensions between you and your spouse?

Sexual: Did the frequency of love-making decline? Did your enjoyment of love-making suffer? Did you avoid your spouse's sexual advances? Did you have extra-marital affairs? Did you engage in abusive or deviant behavior?

Occupational: Did you lose time from work? Was the quality of your work affected? Did co-workers notice your distress? Was your career advancement affected? Were family finances affected?

6. Take Step One: Use relaxation techniques, meditation or prayer to prepare yourself (see Chapter Eleven for help on meditation and prayer). After you have released the worries and anxieties of the day, read over your Step One journal entries. Then repeat your own version of the following affirmation:

I admit that I am powerless over _____, my spouse. I understand that I am unable to change him/her.

I realize my marriage problems are unmanageable by myself alone. I love and respect my spouse unconditionally just as he/she is, just for today. I surrender my claim of trying to change him/her more to my liking, one day at a time. I hereby surrender my struggle to resolve his/her character defect. I release myself from responsibility for the resolution of this character defect to him/her and to God.

This affirmation may be repeated as often as needed.

$\boxed{2}$

BELIEF

STEP TWO: WE CAME TO BELIEVE THAT A POWER GREATER THAN OURSELVES COULD RESTORE US TO SANITY.

If you have genuinely admitted powerlessness over your partner, there may be a certain sinking feeling in your heart right now. The Marital Needs Inventory makes you aware of your needs that are unfulfilled. Resentment yields only bitterness. So you're willing to give that up. But with the surrender comes a sense of aimlessness or hopelessness.

By means of Step One you have gotten in touch with the roots of your resentment. The hopes and dreams you held out for your life and for your relationship with your life partner are mired in conflict and bitterness. Everything you have tried so far has failed. Your marriage is completely unmanageable.

It wasn't always this way. When you first fell in love with your partner, you knew what you wanted, where you were headed, and who you wanted by your side. During that romantic period there was also a fire within you for your own life, a strong, powerful expectancy about the future. That, too, is dimmed by the strain in your marriage. Before you can do something constructive about your marriage you will need to allow your own fire to be rekindled.

Think back to the time when you first met your spouse. Part of Step One was to remember and trace the beginning of the conflict. Now call to mind the qualities of your spouse that first attracted you. Try to remember exactly how you felt about your first date. How did you feel about yourself and your life's direction at that time? Your spouse-to-be had what it took to capture your heart. You were excited at the possibility that he or she would want to be with you. When you were accepted and loved it was one of the most powerful and important experiences in your life. You were full of hope for the future. God—if you believed in God—was definitely on your side. Even if you did not believe in God, the universe seemed friendly and positive. Somehow it was true fate that you would be happy—someone was watching over you.

Somehow that happy time has gone, and right now it looks like it may never return. God must have abandoned you along the way, and all is not right with your world. The feeling of being safe, protected, and watched over is gone.

What happened? You are stuck in a relationship where some of your deepest heart-felt needs and wants remain unfulfilled. Your partner stubbornly refuses to even try. God, or whatever Power there is in the universe, has fated you to be involved with your partner with the faults and character defects that hurt you over and over again.

YOUR CONCEPT OF A HIGHER POWER

The Twelve Step program is a spiritual program, although it is non-sectarian. The real aim of your Twelve Step work is to foster a spiritual awakening—a complete renewal of your whole being: body, mind, and spirit. Your personal concept of a power greater than yourself is important if you seek such a spiritual awakening. If you have ever experienced a profound spiritual experience in your life, this is the time to get back in touch with it. If you have not, there is no time like the present to develop your spirituality.

Like love, it is easy to consider God from an abstract point of view. However, like love, God is only real to you when you experience Him. That is why Step Two is needed; you must make a conscious effort to allow God into your life and marriage.

Now it is quite possible that you or your spouse has already appealed to God as the reason why one of you needs to change. People very often turn to God when they are having serious problems. They quote the Bible, warn of God's displeasure with this or that, and so on. Everyone wants a higher authority to back them up. It gives their complaints credibility. The problem is an appeal to ideals or values can also be a foil used by the controlling mind to win an argument. There is a big difference between "I know what God wants" and "God wants what I want!"

When religion, philosophy, and psychology are used as attempts to fully explain the variety of human experience in some kind of comprehensive whole, they become a means to gain control. They try to make sense of the uncontrollable mystery of life. Religion and philosophies can explain away the impact of life experiences, and no matter what happens you have an explanation for everything.

Trying to dispel the cloud of uncertainty is what makes the appeal to lofty values such a valuable tool for the controlling mind. The choices you have to make in real-life situations are not always easy or clear. You have to make your best call. This often creates anxiety. Terms like *fairness* and *the right thing to do* are difficult to agree on any time, let alone when your feelings are hurt or you are angry. In the heat of an argument, when there is fear or pain involved, one person may use God as a foil to gain an edge on the other. In these situations God is often used by husbands and wives to justify the most outrageous behavior. What sense then, you may ask, does it make to bring God into this?

The problem is not God but *which God?* It is said that man is created in God's image. But the opposite can also be said. God is often perceived as an extension of the things you value and believe in. This always makes an appeal to God suspect when it applies to the expectations of anyone other than yourself.

As a child you may have been given certain impressions by your parents, Sunday school teachers, and the like. Much of our spiritual formation as children is a function of discipline rather than actual spiritual experience. You will want to make a distinction between your impressions of God based on your experience and those ideas about Him you have formed in other ways. With regard to your ideas about God, are they part of your belief system or just ideas you have picked up from others?

Many people were reared with the view that God is a great judge and authority in the sky somewhere who knows every mistake and sin and will punish each one. From this point of view, a merciful and loving side to God may be fleetingly acknowledged, but far more emphasis is placed on His role as the ultimate law giver, rule maker, and punisher of evil doers. And, since every child breaks rules at one time or another, God becomes associated with guilt, punishment, and fear. This concept of God paints a vengeful, uncaring power who allows much evil in the world and lies in wait to punish evil doers in this world and the next.

The barriers to belief in a Higher Power usually involve fear or guilt. The fear that keeps you from a full spiritual awakening has to do with the doubt, anxiety, distortion, and guilt you rejected as a child if you experienced a negative form of belief in a Higher Power. This is often taught as a way of instilling fear and guilt, and was used as a way of getting you to follow the rules and become a "good citizen."

The barriers to belief include your fear that to open the door to a belief in God would mean opening the door to all of the negative beliefs you were taught by your parents and other adults who may have tried to shove "faith" down your throat. You would have to start going to church. You would have to start feeling guilt. You would have to start worrying whether you are going to heaven or to hell.

The fact is that to get back in touch with your spiritual self, you do not have to do or believe any of those things. The Twelve Step program does require belief in some power greater than yourself. While most people choose to call this power "God," the program does not shove any particular belief down your throat. The god of your program is God as you understand Him. No more; no less.

Gather your spiritual beliefs together. You will need them to get you through this crisis.

CAME TO BELIEVE

If you dare to believe in a power greater than yourself, what kind of god would your God be? This is God as you understand Him, personally. You get to decide what you believe about your God—no one else does. As we begin to talk about God in this book, remember that our beliefs about God are influenced by our experiences, and what we believe about God may be different from what you believe. That's okay. You must come to believe in your own personal way.

We, and many others, believe in a loving, caring, powerful God who has a personal interest in you. But if this is true, how could God allow you to end up in a situation, a troubled marriage, like the one you find yourself in? How can it be His will that you be unhappy, perhaps as your parents were unhappy in their marriage?

If you dare to believe in a loving, caring, powerful God, how can He do a miracle that would save your marriage? You could pray that God would magically make your spouse into the person you want him or her to be. Maybe you already have. But that doesn't seem to be the way this miracle will take place. You could pray that God would transform your spouse's heart to see and understand you better and so to become willing to learn and change. But if it is possible for God to work a miracle in your spouse's heart, it is also possible for Him to work a miracle in your heart so that you can understand your partner better and you are more willing to learn and change. That is the miracle you seek.

The spiritual awakening you seek for yourself and desire for your partner will result in a transformed marriage relationship. You will know fully what you need and what you want. You will also be empowered to set aside those needs and wants in favor of one another, when necessary, for the greater good of both of you as a couple. This goal will not be easy to achieve. It will not happen overnight. But if you and your spouse diligently and faithfully work the Twelve Step program together, it will happen. Even if you work the program and your spouse does not, you will experience the clarity of vision and spiritual serenity you need to make the important decisions that will come.

Throughout this book we will be using the terms *God* and *Higher Power* interchangeably. As such, they are used only to designate the spiritual power you have come to believe in and actually experience in your life. We have no intention to either promote or dispute any particular religious or philosophical view. The principles outlined here are intended only to help you improve your conscious contact with *the God you do believe in.*

Recognition of a Higher Power who can restore your marriage to sanity counteracts the sinking feeling that comes with admitting powerlessness over a situation. As you look to your marriage for satisfaction of your needs and desires, and as you honestly confront the issues facing you and your partner, your Higher Power represents what you yourselves have not been able to achieve. Through conscious contact with God you will be able to fulfill your needs by working your program.

GETTING YOUR NEEDS MET

You want so much more for your marriage than you have now. And your ideal for the relationship can become reality only if there is change. From your point of view the most obvious change needed is a change in your partner. If only you had enough power to force a change or enough cleverness to manipulate a change, the marriage would improve. But you don't have that power. You are powerless over your partner; only a Higher Power can accomplish this change.

In fact, as you discovered in your Step One work, your making the attempt to force, manipulate, or coerce your spouse is insane. Step Two states that you can be restored to sanity—the self-destructive cycle of trying to control your spouse can be interrupted and eventually ended. Your struggle to control your spouse was fated to fail from the beginning, but the desire is still quite seductive. It seems that the battle could be won if only you were strong enough.

Think back to your Step One work. Which of your needs remain unfulfilled in your marriage? You have tried to get your partner to recognize your need and to fulfill it the way you want it fulfilled. Yet, you failed. You risked sharing your need, but your spouse is against what you want. At these moments, a strong urge to assert control over the situation wells up inside of you. You choose to stop the intrusion upon your will. The situation no longer involves mere differences of opinion. You feel your partner has crossed a border into territory that is extremely important to you. Thus, you feel threatened on a very deep level. You get angry; perhaps you cry. Something like the instinct to survive moves you. You brush the other person back with a defensive comment or worse.

Rarely does the confrontation stop there. You also have a desire to wound or punish your spouse for invading your privacy. If he or she has robbed you of power once, it will likely happen again. The purpose of the argument, then, is no longer to debate an issue but to re-establish protective space, a buffer zone between your spouse and you.

This wounding or punishing comes out in various ways: tone of voice, sarcastic remarks, abusive language or gestures. Essentially the purpose of the statement is to put down—put down the other person in order to build up yourself and maintain your power in the relationship.

Your will to control causes you to try to bring about a specific action from your spouse. It distorts the way you think. None of us will deny, for example, that we have faults. That would be just too crass. Still, when it comes to giving specific examples of our own imperfections, most people are hard pressed. The will to control always tries to justify its own behavior, and it can make what you fight about seem rather silly to outsiders. But because the issue is linked to your vital needs, it does not seem silly to you.

The will to control is defense oriented. It starts with the natural tendency to protect yourself from hurt and violation of your independence as a person. However, it can work against you. Excessive control comes from the belief that the power to secure your own happiness depends on you alone. In Step Two you will recognize it doesn't depend on you alone. Love is a power greater than you alone that can bring you to greater happiness. Love can fulfill your needs.

TRUST

What makes an issue important enough to fight over is your belief in the power it gives you. The issue serves some purpose or need.

Jerry and Therese have been married for fifteen years. Over the course of their marriage Jerry felt he had gone from disappointment to disappointment, although he had succeeded at everything he tried. He was a successful businessman with three kids, a big house, and a wife who truly loved him, even though he found it hard to believe that she did. Each time he reached another level of success he thought it would fill up the emptiness he felt inside.

At times he wanted nothing to do with Therese. At other times, it seemed vital to have Therese there to affirm him and cuddle him. If he came home to find Therese was out, he became angry. But when she was home, he ignored her or belittled her.

Jerry's anger was a cover-up for his own feelings of emptiness and inadequacy. He avoided his feelings by exercising control over Therese and his children. When directed toward his children, control made him feel he was being a good father. But since Therese was a mature adult, she did not need or want to be controlled by him. Each time she resisted his attempts to control her, he was confronted by his own inner fears. To avoid this situation, he accused her of being insensitive to him.

Their ten-year-old son, Bobby, was the oldest and most rebellious of their three children. Jerry firmly believed that Bobby needed strong discipline and that Therese was too easy on him. When Jerry tried to control Bobby's behavior, he did so through intimidation. He spanked Bobby, threw Bobby in his room, or verbally berated him. Therese, for her part, was afraid of Jerry in some ways and felt powerless to intervene in these episodes. After each one, Bobby hated and feared Jerry more and more and Therese felt she was under criticism from Jerry in the same way as Bobby.

The present crisis in your marriage raises similar questions of trust and fidelity. Trust, forgiveness, and going along with your partner's wishes deliver a certain amount of power to your partner. Yet trust is the condition that makes a marriage relationship possible. This is the great dilemma: *The will to control is diametrically opposite to the movement toward unity and intimacy.* To build trust you have to give up control. Giving up control requires faith.

Whenever you begin a relationship, you choose to allow that person to affect you. You permit that person to "get under your skin," to cross over a boundary into your private sphere. You let another into your world because his or her presence delights you so. It gives you life. The other person gives you a gift of something you cannot obtain on your own. Even when it feels like "magic" brought you together, you make the choice to let that person into your life.

To the degree that you exercise power over that person, you disallow your spouse to act freely. To the degree that you choose not to exert control over the other person, you permit your partner to be who he or she really is, rather than who you want this person to be. You also allow yourself to be seen as you really are. The combination of freedom and vulnerability is the condition that allows love and respect to grow between you.

Letting go of control, however, is fearful because of the freedom you allow your spouse to have. He or she is free to be angry, hurt, understanding, or even indifferent. But, the openness of trust is the invitation to your spouse to be as honest and as authentic as you are.

The hope of romance is for unconditional trust and the freedom to surrender yourself to someone else's care. When you first fell in love you idealized your partner and opened yourself in trust. It was exciting to be accepted unconditionally. There were no strings, and no requirements—only acceptance.

When conflicts and resentments grow, trust decreases. If your partner made promises to change and failed to follow through, your trust diminishes even further. The result is a realistic but discouraged assessment of your spouse. No matter how sincere the promise to change may have been, in some significant areas you find your partner is not trustworthy because of his or her character defects.

You can trust your partner in many areas of life, but when it comes to his or her character defects, you simply cannot trust him or her. You would be setting yourself up for disappointment if you expected your partner to act differently in these situations. It has happened too often before. Your needs and desires are related to your partner's character defects. These defects render him or her unable to meet your needs and desires. These needs and wants are the very areas of your life you must learn to hand over to God and trust that He can and will provide. This may sound like a simplistic and inadequate response to your needs. Yet, it lies at the heart of how your own controlling mind steps into a situation to distort your powers of reason and choice.

How can God provide for your need for affection, security, understanding, warmth, or sexual fulfillment? You have hoped that God would provide these needs through your spouse, and you still believe it is possible since you have not divorced. That belief is what is important right now, at the darkest hour of your marriage. If you have searched your soul and you believe in your heart that your marriage can work, then you have enough faith to continue. The Twelve Step process you have undertaken will strengthen and renew your spirit, no matter what the eventual outcome.

Faith is that quality of the human spirit that can move ahead even in the uncertainty of the future. It flies in the face of what you fear most. It counters control and manipulation so as to experience the truth, whatever it may be. Faith is a necessary quality for the development of wisdom. Like hope, faith does not guarantee the outcome will be what you want or imagine. Faith does not have all the answers. It is, though, the willingness to try and discover the answers. It is the decision to see it to the end, until the conclusion is clear.

Now that the crisis in your marriage commands your attention, it confronts you with an experience of your own powerlessness. Step Two asks you to undergo such an experience, rather than trying to avoid it. In choosing not to control your spouse, you experience him or her as this person really is. In considering your own cooperation with the destructive forces in the relationship, you can open yourself to see your spouse's point of view with less defensiveness. Just because your partner differs from you does not automatically imply ill will. If you persevere to the end, you will begin to discover the real dynamics at work in your relationship.

A HIGHER POWER CAN RESTORE SANITY TO YOUR MARRIAGE

When two equally opposing forces meet, they effectively cancel each other. Like a game of tug-of-war, neither person makes much headway unless the other buckles under. When you are at loggerheads with your spouse, the two of you can hit an impasse. You feel like you are getting nowhere. You don't want to give in and neither will your partner. The mere mention of problem areas may stir up such a reaction that solutions seem to be more trouble than they are worth. So, you or your partner buckle under by not bringing up the subject anymore or by caving in to the other's will. Naturally this is going to leave both of you unsatisfied. The problem is how to wrestle with the issues, not with each other. How do you get control over your own life without controlling your partner? What can break this impasse?

If two equal forces are butting up against each other, the only way to unblock the logjam is for a third force to come in and displace one or both of the two forces. For some couples, their irreconcilable differences force them to break off the relationship. In these cases, the greater force is divorce. Divorce, though, is like an amputation. It is severe, completely disrupting, and should be employed only as a last resort. Moreover, like amputation, divorce does not cure the problem. Indeed, it can add to the problem.

Many couples have found that if they first release control of their own lives to God, whom they understand to be a positive, loving Power greater than themselves, the blockage between them shifts. Remember, the will to control stems from the belief that your happiness depends on you to achieve it. But this is only partially true. Good fortune is a result of circumstances as well as hard work. Counting your blessings means you recognize that goodness has sometimes come into your life without your effort. Sometimes good things happen to you in spite of your best efforts. It is a gift. You were in the right place at the right time. God is the foundation upon which you stand and are free to release control over people, places, and events.

A spiritual awakening to God means a shift from self-will to another's will, from being self-centered to God centered. God is the power and wisdom that leads you to your heart's desire. God enables you to achieve what your own limited self is incapable of achieving.

When Jerry and Therese were courting, they experienced all the power and idealism of romance. Their relationship was unlike any either of them had had before. After they were married, the business of integrating this idealism into a day-to-day routine became a challenge.

Therese refers to the first years of their marriage as the "period of materialism." That was when neither of them thought much about spiritual things. They were planning their life together and trying to acquire the material things that go into making a life: a house, a car, secure jobs, and so on.

For Jerry, it was a pragmatic time. Everything he knew about

God seemed to have no connection with his everyday life. All he had been taught as a child in Sunday school had no impact on his job or his family life. He could go to work, come home, mow the grass, sleep with Therese, and do it all without any thought of God. On the other hand, when he needed help or guidance, he was unable to recognize any supernatural force at work. Jerry was not sure whether God existed or not, but it didn't seem to matter.

Looking back, Therese recognized this time in their marriage as a period of intense adjustment. Their arguments were intense, but their love was intense also. They had lots of energy and ambition. Their troubles started when Therese complained that Jerry's desire for sex had grown to be greater than her's. She could not honestly participate in love-making as frequently as he wanted. That kept Jerry uncomfortably distant from her.

When he desired his wife, one of two things would happen. Either she refused, which made him feel rejected, or she accepted, in which case two other possibilities emerged. If they made love, then he wondered if he was imposing himself on her, and that made him feel self-conscious. If she expressed pleasure and he was able to overcome his anxiety, his appetite for sex increased. In either case he was frustrated and felt, "Either way I come out the loser."

Therese felt that sometimes when they were together she was not truly what Jerry desired. It was as though he was just coming in for service. His touches seemed rote and his mind distracted. When she expressed dissatisfaction and a desire for something more personal, Jerry became upset and embarrassed. He would be angry and brood over what to do next. He said he suspected her of having an affair, and he chided her with comments about a wife's duty to her husband. The pressure built between them. However, Therese would not compromise. She was not willing to make Jerry's sexual gratification the center of their relationship.

Most of all, Therese felt lonely. She took care of the kids, including hard-to-handle Bobby. She worked extra hours at her nursing job. She did it all feeling lonely, distant, and criticized by Jerry. At times she felt she was all alone.

When Therese received a promotion she had been working toward for years, she was elated. All the time and effort she put in had paid off. The position of power and prestige felt good. In fact her job had become the only area in her life where she truly felt respected and esteemed. But after several months in her new position, she was overcome with sadness and a sense of futility.

"I worked so hard and so many hours for this position. And it is good to have achieved it. But it is not enough. I want a husband—a real husband. I want harmony in my home."

She broke down and cried as she explained the situation to her pastor. Never had Therese felt so powerless. Despite her best efforts, she had little to show for them where it mattered to her most. She sat alone in the church and prayed. When she walked out it was already dark.

"I looked up at the stars in the night sky as if I had never seen them before. . . ." How simple, so basic, the whole of her life seemed to her at that moment. Therese felt a peace about her. It was as if her whole life was meant to bring her to that moment of awareness, reduced to that moment of clarity. She was a small part of a big universe that was enormous and beyond her comprehension. Still, she knew that God cared about her personally. She felt God's love for her. She knew that her Higher Power wanted her to be happy. Despite everything that had happened, she had a deep sense that everything would turn out all right. Her panic and despair melted away.

The memory of this experience stayed with Therese for many days. She began to consider her ideas about God. That night under the stars she understood that reality exists whether she is conscious of it or not. She had been so wrapped up in her worry and anxiety that she had forgotten to simply enjoy life, to embrace her life as God's gift.

Therese began to pray and meditate to sustain and deepen the sense of serenity she experienced that night. It felt like she had become reacquainted with an old friend. She read the Bible and some spiritual books that had been collecting dust on her shelves. Nothing external had really changed. Jerry still had a temper. Bobby was still difficult to handle. Yet, Therese had an inner peace and serenity that external events could shake but did not take away.

STEP GUIDE: STEP TWO

SPIRITUAL DEVELOPMENT HISTORY

There are many different definitions for the word *spiritual*. You should use your own. Here, spiritual means the energy of your own life and its connectedness to all other things, including God and other people. Every person embarks on a spiritual journey by virtue of personal growth and development to actualize or harness that energy. The destination of each person's journey is fulfillment.

Though it would be foolish to try to define God, for our purposes here, the term refers to a Power greater than yourself, whose chief effect on you is the gathering of your energies—spiritual, mental, physical, and moral. The success of your journey depends on yielding to God as you understand Him. Awareness of the interconnectedness of all people and events brings insight into your own life, wisdom in the decisions you make, and strength to overcome adversity.

The following questions are designed to help you clarify some of your values.

How do you define marriage?

List five qualities that first attracted you to your partner.

List the five best marriages you know of.

Do you rely on your own ability to think of solutions to problems?

What is your concept of God?

List five ways God, as you understand Him, affects your life.

CURRENT SPIRITUAL AWARENESS

Answer the following questions. Remember this Power that is greater than you is your own concept. All that you really need are the willingness to believe that this Higher Power can restore your life to sanity and a truly open mind.

Are you aware of any of the following roadblocks to coming to believe a Higher Power is present in your life?

A. Indifference; B. Self-sufficiency;
C. Prejudice; D. Defiance.

Do you believe marriage has a spiritual foundation? What does this mean to you?

Does God play a part in your daily life? How?

List five things you want from God.

On a scale of 1 to 10, with 1 being despair and 10 being hope, rate your attitude toward your marriage today.

RESTORATION TO SANITY

Restoration to a sane way of life means freeing yourself from the effects of your own self-willed distortions. As you answer the following questions, try to keep an open mind and be as honest as you can.

Do you have any fears in your life today (fear of people, emotional insecurity, financial insecurity, and so forth)? List these fears.

Can you recognize denial in your life? If so, give examples.

Do you believe that the difficulties in your marriage seem more difficult because of the way you think about them?

Are there areas of your life that you feel you cannot control or that you can control very little? What are these areas?

Describe the last experience you had with each of these feelings or attitudes:

A. Anger; B. Resentment;
C. Jealousy; D. Pride.

Do you consider yourself a positive person? In what areas of your life are you positive?

Do you consider yourself a negative person? In what areas of your life are you negative?

Do you believe that a Power greater than yourself can restore you to sanity (soundness of mind)?

Write a summary description of yourself as you see you today. Remember to list your good points as well as your bad ones.

3

SURRENDER

STEP THREE: WE MADE A DECISION TO TURN OUR WILL AND OUR LIVES OVER TO THE CARE OF GOD, AS WE UNDERSTOOD HIM.

The first two steps have taken you from an honest appraisal of your marriage, where you looked at specific ways in which your relationship leaves you unfulfilled, to a belief that there is a Higher Power willing and able to bring serenity and sanity to your life. The strategies you have tried to get your partner to change have failed, but that is because the focus was either on your partner getting his or her way or you getting your way. This will to control caused a stalemate.

Throughout the Twelve Step program you will notice pivotal action steps. At these stages what you have learned and decided are translated into specific actions. Actions always speak louder than words. Resolving marital difficulties is more than just learning to communicate, even though communicating is important. Resolution also means that you will back up your words with sincere actions. This next step, Step Three, has to do with turning your awareness and faith into concrete action.

Trying to maintain perspective during conflicts is not easy. Like a Ping-Pong ball the power bounces back and forth. First your spouse has trouble dealing with something you did or said. Then while your spouse is getting over that, you have a problem with something he or she did or said. When are you supposed to think about your rights and needs, and when do you make concessions to your partner's needs or wishes? How do you keep from hardening your position? How flexible should you be?

The answer to these questions comes through a right relationship, or perspective, between God, your spouse, and you. God is not a means to control your spouse. But neither are you someone who has nothing to say about the kind of relationship your marriage should be.

In the sixteenth century, an astronomer astounded the world with his revolutionary theory. He said the sun and other planets do not revolve around the earth, as most people of that time thought, but the earth together with the other planets revolves around the sun. This new theory was a great and terrible shock for the academics of that time. They had to learn they were *not* the center of the universe.

This story is told to illustrate your need to put God in the center of your conceptual world. When you do, you will experience a spiritual renewal that will restore your marriage. In keeping this perspective, neither you nor your spouse needs to dominate the other by taking responsibility for anyone's life but your own. In a right relationship there is a time for drawing near and a time for letting go. The wisdom to know when to do what comes from keeping your focus on God's power to work in your life and marriage.

This spiritual perspective runs counter to the will to control. Some recognize they are not the center of the universe, but still they wish they were. The quest for domination is strong. The Superman Syndrome says, "Although I am not the center of the universe, I could be if I were strong enough." Here, power in the form of money, status, or influence is the driving motivation. This person evaluates relationships according to their usefulness in achieving power, or control, over others.

Of course there are those who know they are not the center of the universe and that they never will be. They are content to be the center of a little corner of the universe, for example, their family, their friends, or their co-workers. When something disturbs their little corner, the will to control emerges.

Placing God at the center of your life means embracing the paradox that by giving up your self-centered urges, you will restore your life to sanity. By recognizing the way your life interconnects with others, the way you see and interpret what happens to you will change. With this new perspective come new choices.

CHANGE OF FOCUS

In the previous chapter, Therese and Jerry had a conflict over the way they expressed their intimate feelings toward each other. Therese made a valid point. She and Jerry grew and developed at different speeds. For a long time, however, Therese looked down on Jerry. He was not someone who easily shared his thoughts and feelings. He seemed to miss the point of what she tried to say, or at least did not respond as she hoped he would. She did not think she was better than he, just more mature. However, her perspective soon changed.

Therese had a deep faith in God. This stopped her from trying to fix the problems and handle Jerry. "There were a lot of problems in our marriage and I feared we were on the road to divorce. Still, there were signs of hope that I could not ignore. Sure we fought, but Jerry was not intentionally abusive or indifferent to my concerns. I knew he was suffering too. I just could not convince myself that the marriage was hopeless."

Therese took a positive step by sharing her problems with trusted friends and by bringing her struggle to God. "Things got so bad between us, I thought for sure it was over. I believed that any day Jerry was going to walk in and demand a divorce. We weren't speaking to each other except when absolutely necessary. We certainly weren't sleeping together. There was so much tension between us you could cut it with a knife. Each day I woke up and prayed, 'Just get us through today, Lord.'

"Through the months of fighting and turmoil, I was brought by God to the point of being able to release myself from the desire to fix every issue. Before I had felt an urgency to smooth things out and quickly get back to normal. Looking back now, I realize that normal was unhealthy! I needed to do some growing too.

"I saw I was withdrawing from Jerry when I should have been more explicit about my needs. But I was afraid of how upset Jerry might become. I didn't want to hurt him, and I didn't want to spark his anger.

"I came to realize there was something rather phoney in this. I would hint and beat around an issue, trying to get his attention; then I would back off. All I was accomplishing was creating a lot of hard feelings. What I realized was how I was using my pain as a justification for exercising control in my marriage. Jerry was not living up to my expectations and that upset me. I became sulky and quiet.

"Through a combination of prayer and reflection, I began to realize I was getting nowhere. I became depressed and I was tired of it. I had to do something. I knew if I was to make any real change, I had to get my focus off Jerry's shortcomings and on something positive. I had to control my own self-doubts and not flip-flop between condemning Jerry and condemning myself.

"The most difficult part was learning to let Jerry express anger if he was angry. I had to stop running from or avoiding Jerry when he was angry. For some reason I was afraid. I began to focus my attention on God. When I did not run away or get defensive, Jerry could express himself. By standing my ground internally, I could feel my own true feelings begin to emerge, and I could express them. That turned our arguments into productive conversations, at least part of the time.

"The character defects I identified in Jerry that hurt me most were his verbal abusiveness and aggressive way of pushing his point of view. And I had been used to dealing with these character defects in one of two ways. Either I got angry or I acquiesced. At times I would get angry enough to fight Jerry on every point. We would have terrible fights. We'd fight especially about Bobby's behavior. The fights became shouting matches with insults and barbs hurled back and forth, followed by long, cold silences or polite, but distant, communication for three or four days. However we did it, there was never any resolution. Eventually I took a different approach. I would let him have his way just to avoid a fight, always giving in to keep the peace. But it really wasn't peace at all. I was still burning inside. So we would have another explosive fight every couple of months or so."

When Therese started the Twelve Step program, she attempted to admit her powerlessness over Jerry's irritating way of trying to control her and his aggressive way of dealing with the kids. She found giving up her power over him difficult or impossible because so much seemed to depend on her winning Jerry over to her way of thinking. The more she tried to make him understand, however, the worse things got between them.

Therese decided to "let go and let God." After she had gotten back in touch with her spiritual life through prayer, study, and meditation, she felt a serenity that helped her accept the things she could not change about Jerry. She stopped pushing so hard to get him to see her point of view, and she tried her best not to stay angry and sullen when Jerry acted out his character defects.

Therese was surprised at the result. Their marriage problems certainly had not gone away, but the hard edge of tension between them softened. Therese felt that they had moved away from the brink of divorce. At first, however, she was alarmed by her own interpretation of the situation. "Jerry thinks I'm giving in! That's why things are better between us. He thinks I'm backing down and that I'm admitting he is right about everything. Nothing could be further from the truth!"

Therese could feel her serenity slipping away when she thought this way. Her desire to control the situation had sneaked in the back door. In prayer she sought to turn her will and her life over to the care of her Higher Power. Her will said, "God, make Jerry see what he's doing to me and the kids *now!*" Needless to say, God did not answer Therese's prayer the way she wanted Him to. The process of turning her will and her life over to God came moment by moment, one day at a time.

The care of God, as Therese understood it, included His care for her welfare and her kids' well-being. She painfully concluded that if Jerry still asserted control and was excessively critical toward the kids after a year's time, it would probably be best for her and the kids if she and Jerry separated. Yet Therese had hope that as she worked her Twelve Step program and became less controlling, more detached, serene, and assertive, Jerry would respond favorably to the challenge they faced.

She stopped focusing on whether Jerry was changing and concentrated on herself. Most of all she began to take the time to care for herself in ways she had not done for a long time. One of the most helpful things she did for herself was attend a Twelve Step meeting regularly.

SURRENDER

Much of the strength of the controlling mind comes from your honest desire to improve your relationship and the quality of your life. The controlling mind, though, turns that plan into a demand. Step Three says that this tendency can be corrected only by a surrender to God. God is someone you know to be trustworthy and capable of restoring your life to health and serenity. Your own will submits to the authority of that Higher Power in the realization that your own limited will and understanding are insufficient to achieve what your heart desires most.

With the help of God you can find the solutions to your marriage problems. God can bring about the changes you cannot achieve. Nothing you say or do will open the eyes of your spouse unless God allows it to happen. Similarly, your own controlling mind will distort your thinking unless you surrender it to God.

The word *surrender* means to turn power over to another voluntarily. Taking Step Three means relinquishing control of your life and the desire for control over your spouse, as well as other people and events. What follows is an awakening, a restructuring of attitudes and emotions. The benefits of surrendering your will to God are serenity and wisdom. In a state of surrender your attitude becomes like an open hand, ready to gather whatever comes past it. Through the steady discipline of prayer and meditation your mind and heart remain open and alert rather than closed, possessive, and afraid.

In return for your surrender, expect a new understanding about your marriage. Remember, all things are possible with God, even reconciling the irreconcilable. The God who seemed so hidden before will emerge in everything and everyone. Like planets in the solar system revolving around the sun, you and your spouse will always be independent of one another, each on your own course. You are unique individuals with your own destinies. On the other hand, your common attraction to God—like the attraction of the planets to the sun—draws you into a relationship with each other. At times, therefore, you will be very close to one another, and at other times rather distant. The wisdom that comes from perseverance in yielding to God is that it will inevitably return you to each other's side.

Therese made a firm resolution to give her marriage to God. Once she had decided, she experienced a feeling of darkness. It was at times fearful. It was tearful. She felt like she was becoming even more powerless. She wondered if she was doing something stupid by having hope that the marriage could be restored. Friends told her she didn't have to put up with what she did. They said, "No one has to suffer the way you do."

For Therese it was not abuse that she suffered by turning her marriage over to God, but the loss of the distortions produced by her controlling will. Her sight was being restored to twenty-twenty. She was willing to abandon the quest for control. At the same time she was aware of a growing tranquility. The burden of all the responsibility she had taken was fading away.

"At those moments when I think my perspective is becoming clearer—that is when I want to put myself back into the center of things. I become concerned again for what will happen to me if things do not work out. At the very moment I try to let God take over, that is when I want to reassume control the most."

TURN IT OVER

The life of faith and surrender is a journey of darkness and uncertainty. But that's the way life is. No matter how well planned things are, there is still so much unknown that every day is a journey of faith. In living by faith will you have any guarantees that things will turn out the way you want? No. Each day you will try to regain control over your spouse. You will be checking to see if your spouse is improving or not. Each day you will have to surrender your life and marriage to God. You will have to make this step a daily choice in order to keep the focus on God's will for you.

Turn your will and your life over to the care of God as you understand Him. Even if you believe in a loving and powerful God, this is a scary thought. God has allowed both you and your partner to have free will. If you turn your will and life over to the care of God, what guarantee do you have that your spouse will ever do the same? None. Your spouse may even profess to have already done that. But the process of turning one's life and will over to the care of God is a lifelong project, which no one ever fully and perfectly completes.

Since you have admitted your powerlessness over your spouse, it is obvious that the project of your partner's yielding his or her will and life to the care of God is also not under control. Yet it does affect you. Every day that passes you are tempted to check up on your partner's progress and to assess whether he or she is acting out personal character defects less and less. God can heal your spouse of these offensive character defects. But He does not do it on your timetable. And there is a possibility that your partner may never open up to the degree necessary for growth and transformation to occur. If your partner has a life-controlling problem, such as an addiction to a drug or a compulsive behavior, and remains unrecovered from the addiction, you must face the real possibility that the destructive behavior will continue. But even if your partner is an unrecovered addict, there is hope in the Twelve Step program. Untold thousands of alcoholics have come into the Twelve Step program of Alcoholics Anonymous after their spouses began their own Al-Anon Twelve Step program. Although you cannot control your spouse, what you do affects your partner for better or for worse, making it all the more important for you to work an effective Twelve Step program yourself.

Turning your will and your life over to the care of your Higher Power may be more difficult than you think. If you dare to trust that Power, you may also experience fear of rejection. Your low self-esteem challenges the idea that a Higher Power is interested in you, your life, and your problems. Turning your spouse and your marriage over to God is difficult because this is the area of your life that is most out of control. Mistrust in other areas of life can keep your Higher Power from having a meaningful place in your life as a whole. As you face the most difficult challenge of your life so far, you are faced with the reality of trusting God. In the past prayer may have been an exercise in wishful thinking— asking God as you would your own personal genie to grant what you want. Turning your will and your life over to God's care creates a different, more mature relationship. Since you cannot manage your life by yourself, you need a new and more powerful manager. And it may be quite difficult at first to separate self-will from guidance. Your relationship with your Higher Power will deepen as you become more aware of His presence in the encouraging words of a friend, the inspirational message of a book, or the sense of clarity you may receive in prayer. *Patience* is the watchword as your personal spirituality grows. There is no way to force your own spiritual growth.

The expression "let go and let God" is a simple summary of Step Three. After you have done all that you can to improve your marriage and yourself, it is important to let go and trust God for the outcome. When you are able to fully surrender the burden of responsibility for making things turn out the way you want, you will experience the power and freedom that come from self-acceptance and surrender to God. You are not in charge of your life anymore. Your Higher Power is.

The great paradox of the Twelve Step program is that the less you try to manage your marriage and your life, the more effective you will find yourself becoming. Of course you will still be unable to directly affect your partner's behavior. But as you let go of the responsibility to solve your marriage problems all by yourself, the more peaceful and serene attitude that comes with surrender will help you to see your part more clearly. You will feel the weight of a burden lifted from your shoulders. You are not responsible for saving your marriage! You are only responsible for working a good program one day at a time.

STEP GUIDE: STEP THREE

The following exercises will help you clarify your present belief in God and His power to help you. Write the answers to these questions in your journal.

1. List five ideas about love you had as a child, as an adolescent, and now as an adult.

2. List five ideas you had about God as a child, as an adolescent, and now as an adult.

3. Do you recognize any changes or patterns? For example, have you become more or less skeptical, sophisticated or simple, satisfied or confused about these matters?

4. Where are the best places for you to go to gather your thoughts and energies when you are feeling scattered or frazzled?

5. When is the best time for you to recollect yourself?

6. Do you feel that you are now truly willing to turn your life and marriage over to the care of God as you understand Him? Explain.

7. What are five things you believe God can do for your marriage?

An important prayer used by people in Twelve Step programs clearly sums up the intentions of the person taking Step Three. It is called The Serenity Prayer:

God, grant me the serenity to accept the things I cannot change, courage to change the things I can, and the wisdom to know the difference. Thy will, not my will be done.[1]

This prayer could be recited whenever you feel the urge to seize control of a situation, when you need help in making a decision, or when you experience the limitations of your own power.

Take Step Three by reciting aloud the following prayer or one like it with a spiritually empathetic person.

God, I offer myself to You to build me and do with me as You will. Relieve me of the bondage of self, that I may better do Your will. Take away my difficulties, that victory over them may bear witness to those I would help of Your Power, Your Love, and Your Way of Life. I want what You want.[2]

The more sincerely you can utter these words, the greater your satisfaction and progress will be.

4

MORAL INVENTORY

> **STEP FOUR: WE MADE A SEARCHING AND FEAR-LESS MORAL INVENTORY OF OURSELVES.**

The experience of powerlessness over your spouse takes on a more specific shape as you begin to make your way through the steps of acceptance and surrender (Steps One, Two, and Three). Now, you are beginning to recognize the specific areas in which you feel powerless and the specific traits in your spouse that trigger this feeling in you.

As you have come to the awareness of your powerlessness, you have also become aware of God's gentle hand in this Twelve Step journey. Paradoxically through the turbulence of working out troubles in your marriage and within yourself, you can begin to feel a growing sense of security and serenity. You begin to experience the sensation of movement, healing, and growth. You may still feel anxious; your problems have not gone away. However, as you are truly letting go and letting God take over your relationship, you begin to develop a sense that your attitudes, moods, and thought patterns are headed in a new direction. This growing assurance will help you as you continue in your recovery. The same honesty, openness, and courage you employed in the first three steps will be required of you in the awareness and transformation phase (Steps Four through Nine).

Step Four is the heart of this awareness and transformation. A well done, successful Step Four will be the key to revitalizing your marriage.

You may be asking yourself, "Why should I make an inventory of my entire life and all my affairs? The problem is the marriage. So, why don't I just take inventory of the relationship?" The answer to this question lies in the fact that in a healthy marriage relationship there is an implied but unspoken contract between a husband and wife. The first part says, "I would like you to help me work through my unresolved childhood conflicts."[1] The second part is similar, "I am willing to help you work through your unresolved childhood conflicts." This contract is based on the nature of marriage itself and upon the chemistry that exists between the two of you.

Part of the excitement of a new romance is the belief that within the love relationship you can expect complete and total acceptance. As you build trust, you are inclined to disclose more and more of yourself to your (future) spouse: your dreams, secret desires, and personal goals. Thoughts occur to you like, "I can tell him everything," and "I know she accepts me for who I am." Within this atmosphere of trust and acceptance, you both let down your defenses, and the unfinished business of growing up is finished. Through this intimate interaction, you begin to resolve questions of personal worth, ability, future security, and well-being, as well as past conflicts. Your spouse becomes close enough to you to understand your personal unfinished business and innermost conflicts. Throughout courtship, sometimes all the way to the altar, couples may ask themselves, "Is this the one?" But the real unspoken question is, "Is the person I have chosen as my life partner the one who will help me become the complete, wholly developed person I am meant to be and want to be?" Marriage is intended to be no less than the nurturing environment necessary for you to reach full maturity.

That you picked this particular person has to do with *chemistry*. What is *chemistry?*

When your romance began, you idealized your partner. He was the most exciting person you had ever met! She was unlike any other woman you had ever known before! What made your future spouse appear so different from all the others? It was the way he or she embodied the traits, values, and lifestyle in your ideal of what a husband or wife should be. This ideal derives from your own background.

From the beginning, you were bound to be attracted by your spouse, or someone with similar qualities, because you are naturally attracted to a partner who has some of the same character traits as your parents. You didn't go to school to learn how to be a husband or wife; you picked up these ideas from your environment. Men are often attracted by women who have some traits that their mothers possessed, and they have often incorporated a number of their fathers' personality traits into their own characters. Women are also attracted to men who have some traits similar to their fathers'. They also may have acquired some qualities similar to their mothers' traits. Chances are your spouse will notice this before you do and make a comment like, "You remind me of your mother (or father) when you do that."

Not all the aspects of this idealized spouse are necessarily ideal, particularly when hurts, rejection, feelings of inferiority, and shame have been part of your family history. Unconsciously you may feel a sense of excitement and opportunity. Here is a chance to relive some of those hurt-filled experiences and "make things right." You may select a marriage partner because he or she is imperfect in just the right way.

Many partners in troubled marriages come from families where emotional pain and hurts were not dealt with effectively. In fact, most families have some form of *dysfunction* present within the family system. Alcoholism, for example, affects one in five families! Adult children of alcoholics (also known as ACOAs) invariably have deep-seated hurt as a result of growing up in an alcoholic home. Alcoholism is known as a family disease. It is not any one individual who is to blame. Rather it is the family system that needs to be healed.

However, you don't have to be an ACOA to have serious and unresolved conflicts still within you from your upbringing. Any time one family member has a serious problem, be it an addiction of some kind or any sort of consistent emotional problem (such as chronic depression), the whole family chemistry is affected. Some people are under the impression that if troubles occur when they are younger they will get over them in time. But that is not so. Children are particularly sensitive in their formative years and are least likely to be aware of the impact of their family environment. Children are not sophisticated enough in their thinking to comprehend their parents' emotional problems. In fact, they idealize their parents and cannot distinguish between, for example, Daddy's anger because he is frustrated with the child's behavior and Daddy's anger because he is frustrated by problems of his own. That is why early childhood hurts run so deeply and can remain unconsciously active for years, becoming so completely a part of the personality that the adult has trouble acknowledging the presence of these deep-seated hurts.

Another common dysfunction in the family is the "rageaholic" parent who cannot moderately express anger or disapproval. Sometimes the rageaholic has other problems, such as alcoholism, though not always. Anger and power over the family are "the drugs." Everyone in the family knows that and tiptoes around the rageaholic in order to avoid the rage.

Sometimes the dysfunction in a family is actually just the encounter with a novel experience that demands the development of an otherwise unused skill. You may have had a very pleasant childhood and have a very loving relationship with your own family. When you marry your spouse, however, the chemistry changes sufficiently to expose areas in your own maturity that need developing or strengthening. A woman who experienced a protected and nurtured childhood, for example, may lack certain assertiveness skills. A strong-willed husband can overpower her if she does not learn to adjust to this new experience. Your interpersonal development may not have been dysfunctional but simply unfinished.

It is your unfinished business of maturing that colors your perception of your spouse, and so the idealization of your spouse at the beginning of your relationship gives way to what has been called the "Grand Reversal."[2] What were once very attractive qualities in your spouse, for example, being carefree, exciting, flexible, generous, and bold, may now be viewed as irresponsibility, unreliability, disorganization, wastefulness, and insensitivity. Although neither portrait is completely accurate, since both are so absolute, the Grand Reversal occurs because childhood conflict or underdevelopment carries over into your adult relationship with your spouse. The same feelings of powerlessness and rage, or emptiness and hurt, that you may have experienced as a child are the roots of the current issues being dealt with in the face of your spouse's defects.

The accumulation of unresolved conflicts, stored-up hurts, and learned habits of interrelating is sometimes referred to as "emotional baggage." The one you have selected as your life partner is also the one you have selected to help you unpack this baggage, that is, to dispose of these unresolved issues. The thing to remember, however, is that the primary responsibility for working through these issues is yours, and yours alone. This is what Step Four is all about: taking this responsibility head on and not dumping it on your spouse. How do you go about this?

The focus until now has been on dealing with (or, in a certain sense, *not* dealing with) your partner's shortcomings, instead of turning them over to your Higher Power. In Step Four, the focus turns to your own character with its particular strengths, or virtues, and its weaknesses, or defects.

These personality traits are the means by which you cope with reality, or what happens to you. You are conscious of some aspects of your character and not of others. Some qualities work for you and others do not. That is, your character traits either aid you in reaching your goals or they hinder you. The purpose of a moral inventory is for you to become conscious of both what is working for you and what is working against you. What is "moral" is what serves to fulfill you as a complete, wholly developed person. What stifles or prohibits the realization of who you are is "immoral." In a later step, you will learn how to remove the self-destructive traits. Step Four is concerned only with being able to distinguish between the two.

The difficult part of Step Four is staying on task. As a partner in a troubled marriage, you are acutely aware of your partner's character defects and exactly how they hurt you. In Steps One, Two, and Three, you were asked to let go of your spouse's character defects and to let God and your spouse handle them. Now, Step Four suggests looking at your own character defects. And it's not easy! For one thing, your spouse probably focuses enough on your faults for the both of you, right? And for another, why should you do what he or she is unwilling to do? Well, the reason is simple: It is best for you and your marriage to do it.

The "Big Book" of Alcoholics Anonymous says that character defects are part of the acquired false self from instincts that are misdirected. In Troubled Couples Anonymous the concept of unfulfilled needs and emotional baggage is closely related to the idea of the "acquired false self." As you grow up, hurtful experiences combine to teach you certain lessons. You form certain impressions about the world, other people, and your own individual needs. A particular character trait of, say, your mother may be so annoying and distasteful that you have promised yourself you will never be like her in that way. However, the trait will very likely emerge in you unless you consciously change it. Even then, you will tend to slip back into your parent's pattern. Why? Because that is the way you first learned how to deal with people. That is what seems normal and comfortable to you. Everything involved in family life, from arguing to financial decisions to parenting style, was modeled in your family. That is the norm you work from, even if it was dysfunctional or destructive.

An instinct may be described as a set of behaviors designed to fulfill a need. A misdirected instinct is a well-intentioned effort to fulfill one's need in a particular area. The results are poor because the acquired, or learned, pattern of behavior is ineffective or counterproductive. For example, one basic human need is for respect—both self-respect and respect from others. If a man grew up in a home where his father sought to fulfill his need for respect by constantly demanding it from everyone around him, this man would grow up believing the only way to be truly respected is by constantly demanding displays of respect from others and becoming enraged if it is not properly paid. It will take a change in his basic belief about respect and how to get it for him to be able to adjust his behavior to be more effective in gaining respect in his marriage relationship.

Understand that character defects exist in everyone. They are part of the unfinished business of maturing or growing up, no matter how old you are. Recognition of a defect need not be an occasion for embarrassment or shame. There are many reasons for these deficiencies, most of which are not consequences of someone's evil intent but of a dysfunctional family system. If a behavior or belief is frustrating the fulfillment of your life's project of happiness it needs to be analyzed and restructured. This point cannot be emphasized too much. The moment you begin to see one of these deep character traits surface, you will find yourself defending it, even though it is hurting you. This should show you how deeply rooted it is and how fully it has colored your sense of right and wrong, good and bad.

The agony and strife of troubles within your marriage pose for you a unique situation, one that deserves a moment's consideration. You may be angry with your spouse about particular habits and behaviors. Yet, the confrontation draws out the defects in your own character that are products of intergenerational turmoil, sickness, and disease. The troubles are only symptoms, the pain only the alarm that signals something has gone wrong.

Here you have an opportunity to attend to the heart of the problem and be truly and completely healed. It is a matter for your own conscience to decide whether this is the functional side of that unspoken marriage contract or not. Remember, the implied contract in a healthy marriage says, "I would like you to help me to work through my unresolved childhood conflicts, and I will do the same for you." Your spouse is the well-suited partner who can help you uncover and dispose of some of the emotional baggage that remains a part of you. Your spouse is "well-suited" for the task because of the unique way in which the two of you fit together. You call sickness and disease out of each other in order to expel them with loving compassion. Your individual backgrounds and personalities combine to affect one another in a particular way. If your wife draws out some of your worst qualities, divorcing her will not remove those qualities from you. She may be the catalyst by which God cures you of your deepest wounds. Perhaps the greatest gift of your marriage is its power to hold you to the task of growing into your own maturity.

SEAN AND JENNIFER

Sean and Jennifer's story illustrates how this process of healing begins. They fight all the time. They dated for two stormy years, fighting and making up continually during their courtship. The thing that kept their relationship going was how great they felt when they made up after a big argument. The problem was that each fight was more explosive than the last, until on a few occasions the verbal fighting erupted into physical violence. Fights would end with a slap, grabbing about the shoulders or forearms, or even a push or a shove.

On the evening of her birthday, Sean took Jennifer out for dinner at her favorite restaurant. "We were talking and having a pleasant evening," he says. "Then the subject of my recent trip to visit my mother after her surgery came up. Jennifer complained that I should have told her further in advance that I intended to go. But the suddenness of Mother's illness was such a shock to me, and Jennifer and I had been fighting so much, that I just didn't feel like talking to her about it. Then she complained that I hadn't confided in her about making the trip and that she wanted to help me but felt I had 'shut her out.'

"I know she was just trying to help, but it seemed so selfish to me that she thought more about her own feelings than mine in that kind of situation. When she went on about the way I was brought up and how it had seriously affected our relationship, that was the last straw for me.

"Even though I knew she was trying to be positive and work on our relationship, I couldn't help saying exactly what I thought: 'You don't care about my mother. You never have cared about her. You use every situation to gain advantage for yourself. Every one! It doesn't matter to you if my mother is sick or well!' Well, that opened Pandora's box. Jennifer started in on how I was so selfish and concerned about how much attention I was getting when her father was ill and dying. She was so angry that she opened the car door to get out while the car was moving! I grabbed her around the shoulders to restrain her and she fought me all the more."

Jennifer and Sean came from two entirely different family backgrounds. That made it difficult for them to understand each other's character traits. Jennifer was brought up in an Italian family rooted in their ethnic heritage. She enjoyed the chivalrous attitude of the men in her world. She liked being treated as special—having doors opened for her and such—but she wanted to adopt the independence and flexibility of being a modern American woman as well. She saw herself as passionate, hot blooded, and spoiled.

Sean grew up in an alcoholic home. Although he was never physically abused by his alcoholic father, he was subjected to constant emotional abuse and cruelty. He had a younger sister, Terry, who was disabled and took up most of his mother's time. He learned to be quite independent and somewhat of a loner. He became a computer scientist and relied on his ability to reason things out.

In the climate of hostility and alienation, Sean and Jennifer's sexual relationship was also quite stormy. On the upswing after a fight when they had made up, sex could be great. The passion and emotion of reconciling after a particularly heated fight became a basis for romantic passion and a sense of abandon in their relationship. Without really thinking about it, Sean plunged headlong back into an intense and heartfelt closeness with Jennifer that was sealed and symbolized by their making love. The only problem was that the feeling of closeness did not last long. Tension started to re-build almost immediately because the underlying issues remained unresolved.

SEAN'S ACCEPTANCE AND SURRENDER

Sean began to think about their marriage. He said to himself, "If only she would show me a little respect. She always insists on doing things her way." Sean felt powerless and emasculated. He struggled to put his finger on Jennifer's fault that was most hurtful to him.

"It's not so much the things we argue about like money, sex, closeness, and emotional support that bother me. It's the fact that when we fight she is ruthless and Machiavellian. She'll use anything to make her point, to gain advantage."

Sean then named what he thought was Jennifer's character defect: "She tends to use coercion in our relationship." Sean resolved to let go of his obsession about Jennifer's character defect. He began by examining his own beliefs.

He knew he had grown far from his spiritual roots. His career as a computer scientist conveniently reinforced the survival strategy he had learned as a child: Avoid being hurt by approaching life in an organized, rational way. He met Jennifer at a time when he was trying to break out of that isolated world of his own creation and focus on others.

"When I first met her, Jennifer was going through a rough time, and I wanted to give to her. And she took from me. What I didn't know at the time is that it wasn't just because she was going through a rough time with her father's death. She takes and then takes more. It never stops."

Sean turned over to God and to Jennifer the responsibility for Jennifer's tendency to use coercion to fulfill her needs in their relationship. He no longer saw himself as the one responsible for making her happy. And Sean quickly turned over his desire to fix Jennifer's faults. He fully relinquished this task to his Higher Power, even though he wanted her to get over her problems more than anything else in the world.

Finally Sean was ready to take Step Four. He began by looking at the one character flaw in Jennifer that was most hurtful to him. After careful reflection, he identified this character flaw as "her tendency to use coercion to get what she wants." By reviewing his own life for previous encounters with the same flaw, he realized that the reason this particular character flaw is the most hurtful to him is because of his own unfulfilled needs for a sense of power and influence. That was true in his own family while he was growing up, just as it was true in his relationship with Jennifer.

He then called to mind each person in his life who had ever hurt him. It was not an easy task, because when he started, the only person who came to mind was Jennifer. "This can't be true," he thought to himself. "Perhaps there have been people who have hurt me to a lesser degree." That brought to mind some names. Over the course of two weeks, he thought of a number of people close to him who had indeed hurt him in the past, although almost always the hurt was unintentional.

As he fully and honestly pondered the hurts in his life, he found that he held in his heart much more anger and resentment than he had thought. He realized that he felt angry toward his mother, his father, and his sister, Terry, as well as his wife, Jennifer, but for different reasons.

He was angry at his mother because she was always busy with Terry. She never seemed to have enough time for him. She never seemed able or willing to protect him from the continual criticism, yelling, and screaming his father aimed at him. When he reached out to his mother for support, he found none.

He was angry at his father for all the abuse heaped upon him from the time he was a small child. It seemed to him that as he grew up he could not do anything right. He felt guilty much of the time because his father often said it was his fault his mother was overburdened. He was often told, "You don't help enough with your sister." When he tried to please his father, he found that it was impossible. He was always expected to have done more and to have done it better.

He also discovered he was angry with Terry. Although he knew she was disabled and really could not have known better, Sean realized he resented the way she ruled their home. Whenever she wanted anything, it seemed that the world stopped until she got it. His parents felt so guilty and responsible for her that she was never trained properly or disciplined. She threw tantrums and disrupted the household regularly. Sean never felt free to voice his feelings or do anything about the situation.

Sean recognized his old feelings of powerlessness and rage and a deep longing for something better. He connected these feelings with the current feelings he had toward Jennifer. There were several hurtful incidents he could remember in his childhood and adolescence and several in his early relationship with Jennifer. He wrote more about these in his journal and found that the events formed a pattern. He had felt hurt, angry, and powerless in a number of these situations. He realized that his own character defects of "a tendency to hold on to resentments" and "insensitivity" had their roots in these events. He was reproducing in his own marriage the injustices leveled against him as a child, against which he had raged for many years.

When Sean began his Twelve Step program to improve his marriage, he was centered on Jennifer's anger and coercive attempts to change him and his behavior to be more to her liking. He, of course, resisted her attacks and defended his way of doing things as being reasonable and right. After a while he became very angry and resented her persistent complaining about him and how he had failed to make her feel "special." The more he centered on her character defects, the worse things became.

Although it was quite difficult at first, he let go of his obsession with Jennifer's coerciveness and began the process of looking at his own character defects. What he learned about himself surprised him. His anger and resentment had not begun in his relationship with Jennifer. Rather, his deep-seated hurts had their roots in his childhood and adolescence.

Sean discovered that the hurtful experiences of his childhood had erroneously taught him that anger is an unacceptable emotion. Consequently, he strove to be "calm, rational, and peaceful" in his adult intimate relationships. Conflict, irritation, and disagreement are, Sean thought, to be avoided as much as possible. As a result of this approach to his relationship with Jennifer, Sean experienced many hurts, which early in the relationship he simply ignored. He made excuses for Jennifer: "Her father just passed away. She's under a lot of stress." He never expressed his annoyance or irritation with her. He simply "stuffed" his feelings of anger as he had learned to do in his childhood. When eventually he blew up at Jennifer, he slipped into a mode of venting his anger and frustration in a way that was abusive and destructive. At these times Jennifer would break down and cry while Sean yelled at her. Sean knew, after the fact, that episodes like this were very destructive to the relationship and that Jennifer's hurt and resentment became worse when they happened, but he felt he had no control. Sometimes he just could not take it anymore and he simply had to vent his anger.

Sean recognized that the episodes of venting his anger at Jennifer, even after she had begun to withdraw and cry, were examples of his worst character defects, namely, his tendency to hold resentment, his insensitivity, and his indifference to Jennifer's feelings when he was angry. Sean's Step Four work helped him to place his character defects in proper perspective.

He knew, for example, that in general he did not hold on to resentment. In fact in the majority of his relationships he was quite easy-going and quick to forgive. Only in situations like his relationship with Jennifer, where he felt there was a lot at stake, did he tend to hold resentment. As he thought about the exact nature of his resentment toward Jennifer, which he had already begun to identify in Step One, he realized that his own specific character defects contributed to his anger and resentment toward his wife. He associated the fact that in his childhood he was never allowed to express anger at the time he felt it with the fact that routinely he did not express his anger and annoyance with Jennifer, but allowed resentment to build. The pattern was not universal. It was quite specific. When Sean felt angry at someone he loved, an internal message said, "Stuff it! It's too dangerous to express anger!" He had believed this internal message and adapted his behavior accordingly. He did not share what bothered him most, and so he allowed resentment to build to an explosion.

A moral inventory identifies your character defects as well as your virtues. By definition character defects are destructive to you and your marriage. Virtues, on the other hand, build up both you and your marriage. These qualities within you have their roots in your childhood and upbringing. Once you have identified both your strengths and weaknesses, this awareness helps to transform your view of your marriage problems. While you started out being able to see the problems and their solutions only from the narrow perspective of what your partner should do to change, by recognizing how your own unfulfilled needs color your perspective, you can begin to see what you yourself can do to improve the situation.

Take a look at where your Twelve Step work to revitalize your marriage has brought you. First, you've accepted your powerlessness over your spouse. You've fully acknowledged his or her independence as a person, even though you are married. Next, through a spiritual awakening, you've become aware of God's activity within you and in your marriage relationship. The next step was to surrender your will in all things to your Higher Power. Now, in Step Four, the challenge is to turn that spotlight of yours, once firmly pointed at your spouse, and redirect it toward yourself and your own set of character defects and virtues.

STEP GUIDE: STEP FOUR

In the previous three steps, you built a beginning foundation in your personal program to revitalize your marriage. In Step One, you admitted you were powerless over your spouse and that your marriage problems had become unmanageable. Step

Two raised your awareness that sanity (that is, constructive rather than destructive behavior in your marriage) could be restored through a right relationship with God as you understand Him. In Step Three, you learned that turning your will and life over to the care of God is the best course of action.

At this point, the release of your spouse's character defects to God and to your spouse is in the process of becoming an effective reality. The time has come to take the spotlight off your spouse and place it on yourself. You are face to face with Step Four.

Step Four allows you to uncover your acquired character defects that are destructive to your marriage. As you begin Step Four, it is important that you understand the true nature of these so-called character defects. The most important factor is that these defects were acquired through past experiences. They are ineffective coping skills, and they are, in fact, learned behavior. Because what was learned can be unlearned, the defects are not an indelible part of you or your character. Rather, they are part of a "false self"—a set of unhealthy character traits that has been established as a result of hurtful, painful, and growth-squelching experiences. Awareness of these unhealthy traits and the experiences from which they arise is the beginning of a process of growing out of them. There is a "true self" as well—the set of healthy character traits that were attractive to your spouse in the first place and that enabled you to begin and establish a love relationship with your partner. Step Four will place you in touch with these traits.

In fact as you take inventory using the inventory sheets and various checklists that follow, you will find that each of your character traits is a two-sided coin. One side is the defect—the way the particular character trait can be hurtful to others, especially your spouse. The other side is your virtue—the special ways your character traits can encourage and build up others, particularly your spouse. In the course of completing Step Four, you will work to achieve a balanced, accurate, and realistic view of yourself and your traits.

In Part One you will explore the roots of the character defects you acquired in your childhood, adolescence, and early adulthood experiences. In Part Two, you will expose the current manifestations of these character defects in your marriage relationship.

PART ONE: INVENTORY SHEETS

1. Make a list of everyone in your life who has ever hurt you in chronological order from childhood and on to adolescence and adulthood. Undoubtedly the list will include your parents and other family members, even though the hurts may have been quite unintentional. Make as complete a list as possible. Write your spouse's name last.

2. Fill in a separate five-column Inventory Sheet for each person on your list (see Figure A below). One of Sean's responses is filled in as an example.

FIGURE A: INVENTORY SHEET

Situation	How I Felt Rate 1–100	Lesson Learned (Core Belief)	Acquired Character Defect
PERSON: My dad I wanted to go out for the football team, but when I told my father, he screamed at me, saying I was selfish for leaving my mom alone to take care of my sister in the afternoon. He said I was self-centered, good-for-nothing and that all I ever thought of was what I wanted.	Angry – 90 Guilty – 80 Frustrated – 100 Sad – 75	1. Keep your mouth shut. 2. Stuff your anger to avoid punishment. 3. If you want something badly you won't get it. 4. Try to forget about what you want. 5. My dad has withdrawn his love because I'm unworthy of his love.	Non-assertiveness Stuffing anger Resentment Sense of inadequacy Low self-esteem Toxic shame

3. Reflect on your journal entries as Sean did. Find the patterns in the hurtful situations that you have experienced and how the lessons you learned in those incidents have resulted in your specific character defects.

4. Look over your list of faults and pick out the ones that you believe are most hurtful to your spouse. Write them down and begin Part Two to take inventory of exactly how they are manifested in your marriage relationship today.

PART TWO: CHECKLISTS

Below are a number of *need values.* They represent ingredients for a happy, fulfilled relationship. The exercise of particular virtues helps to bring this need value into existence in your life. The defects help to drive it out. Odd-numbered items in the checklists represent manifestations of the character defect. Even-numbered items illustrate the opposite virtue as it occurs in your behavior and in your attitude toward your spouse. Describe in your journal the last time each of the situations in the checklists occurred. Skip the item if it has never occurred or if you do not remember such an incident.

Need Value: Affection

Affection is a basic human need value. Newborns need affection to survive, just as they need nourishment and shelter. Because affection is such a basic human need, it is hurtful and destructive when it remains unfulfilled. If your upbringing did not fully provide for this need, you may find that the character defect of indifference is a major factor in your marriage.

DEFECT: INDIFFERENCE/WITHDRAWAL

Manifested as an uncaring attitude about right and wrong; an uncaring attitude about people and their welfare, particularly your spouse; an uncaring attitude about God and His will for you.

VIRTUE: INTIMACY/TENDERNESS

Manifested as a loving orientation toward others; a loving, caring, and romantic orientation toward your spouse.

CHECKLIST

1. It came to your attention that you had overlooked a need of a friend, family member, or your spouse that he or she had been depending on you to fulfill.

2. You felt a warm glow, tender feelings, or joy upon seeing your spouse.

3. You became aware that you had overlooked or had been indifferent to a desire of a friend, family member, or your spouse that you had known about but did nothing to meet.

4. You expressed affection for your spouse by using a term of endearment, a loving tone of voice, or some physical contact (such as touching or holding hands).

5. You were told by your spouse, a friend, or a family member that you seem withdrawn, distant, or "wrapped up in yourself."

6. You found yourself concerned about your partner's welfare and expressed your concern with something you did or said.

7. It came to your attention that you have expressed little caring for those in need in your community, that you give little to charitable causes, or that you have not volunteered your help for a charitable organization for a long time.

8. You accept your partner totally (defects and virtues) and you expressed your acceptance of one of his or her character defects in something you did or said.

9. You alienated your spouse because of something you did or something you said.

10. You and your spouse enjoyed each other's company while doing routine things or nothing in particular.

Need Value: Respect

Sean and Jennifer's conflicts exploded into verbal and sometimes physical altercations. Respect restricts the arguments to issues and does not attack the other person or his or her character.

DEFECT: ABUSIVENESS/PASSIVE-AGGRESSION

Manifested as a disrespectful or disparaging attitude toward others and your spouse; a tendency to criticize, degrade or put down others' ideas, actions, or qualities without regard or respect for their point of view; a contrary or negative disposition; nonassertiveness.

VIRTUE: ESTEEM/ASSERTIVENESS

Manifested as the ability to affirm others and your spouse as special, valuable, and worthwhile; willingness to honor, admire, and respect the best in others and in your spouse; the ability to openly and honestly express your needs and wants.

CHECKLIST

1. You made a critical comment to your spouse without thinking and it hurt his or her feelings.

2. When your spouse complained, you took the time to find out exactly what had upset him or her.

3. You became aware that you had been in a bad mood and had been irritable and, as a result, quite critical and intolerant of your spouse during the time you spent together.

4. You expressed an interest in your partner as a person—his or her career, recreation, interests, goals, desires, etc.

5. You made a critical or judgmental comment about your spouse's family.

6. You asked your spouse's opinion about a problem.

7. You planned an activity that you knew would affect your spouse without consulting him or her in advance.

8. You complimented your spouse on his or her ability in an area you knew that he or she is proud of.

9. You made a critical comment about your spouse in front of friends or strangers.

10. You clearly expressed what you want from your spouse on a sensitive issue, such as sex, finances, or parenting.

Need Value: Skill

Fear of the unknown or fear of failing can keep a person from acting effectively and efficiently in relationships. Being overly cautious or pessimistic can doom projects from the start. A little adventurousness can breathe new life and interest into daily routines.

DEFECT: INADEQUACY/INCOMPETENCY

Manifested as inability and failure in areas basic to the marriage relationship; underachievement with regard to career, development of talents and interests; unwillingness to learn and to grow.

VIRTUE: ACHIEVEMENT/COMPETENCY

Manifested as competency and ability in areas most important to the couple in their marriage relationship; development of skill, interests, and talents; achievement of career goals; willingness to meet challenges; creativity.

CHECKLIST

1. Your spouse repeatedly complained that he or she must deal with almost every problem that comes up, such as finances, home-improvement, child care.

2. You took special pride in learning a new skill that benefitted the family (such as how to fix the car, repair plumbing, cook a gourmet dish).

3. You turned down an opportunity to do something new and different with your spouse because you were "too tired," "not interested," or thought it was silly.

4. You and your spouse learned a new recreational activity together (sailing, square dancing, mountain climbing, card games, and so forth).

5. Your spouse, friends, or family observed that you do not take initiative in your career and that you have lost your ambition with regard to your goals.

6. Your enthusiasm for a project caught on with your spouse and he or she was inspired to help.

7. You became aware that you and your spouse are "in a rut" in regard to recreational pursuits and spare-time activities.

8. You decided, with your spouse's support, to take a significant risk in order to advance your career (such as change your job or go back to school).

9. You left an important home-improvement or other project incomplete or you took an excessively long period of time to complete it.

10. You demonstrated your skill or ability in such a way that it was a source of pride to your spouse and your family.

Need Value: Understanding

Understanding requires the coordination of one's mind with one's emotions in order to sustain goodwill through thick and thin. It exercises humility and recognizes that "there but for the grace of God go I."

DEFECT: DISTORTION/INSENSITIVITY

Manifested as a tendency to misunderstand, distort, or confuse your spouse's point of view; uncertainty or ignorance about your spouse's feelings on important issues; distortion of your spouse's intentions.

VIRTUE: EMPATHY/SENSITIVITY

Manifested as sensitivity and wisdom with regard to your spouse's feelings; knowledge of his or her viewpoint, virtue, and character defects.

CHECKLIST

1. You ignored your spouse's point of view on an important decision and went ahead with things as you wanted.

2. You could see through your spouse's eyes, even though you disagreed with him or her, and you let your spouse know that you understood his or her viewpoint.

3. You misinterpreted a situation in which your spouse was with an opposite-sex friend, and you became jealous.

4. When your spouse was feeling down, you found that you could share some of that feeling and you offered support.

5. You found yourself avoiding your spouse because you knew he or she was depressed or in an irritable mood.

6. Your spouse felt able to confide his or her most private thoughts and feelings to you.

7. You simply did not understand what your spouse was so upset about.

8. You identified a sensitive topic or area for your spouse and consciously tried to become more understanding and empathetic in that area.

9. You found out later that your spouse was very distressed in a particular situation that you had known was difficult for him or her (such as a social gathering, family event, before a job interview).

10. You encouraged your spouse when he or she wanted to engage in a new venture, even though it would affect you in some way (such as by costing money, taking up your spouse's time and energy).

Need Value: Power and Influence

Couples often subconsciously exchange tit for tat. The expectation is established that "I will do this for you if you do that for me." You may be unable to discuss certain topics or they may be presumed to be the domain of one or the other. A sense of having full voice or an equal vote in matters big and small comes from the view of marriage as a partnership.

DEFECT: COERCION/RESENTMENT

Manifested as a tendency to overpower, coerce, or dominate your spouse; attempting to force him or her to do things your way; subtly trying to influence or manipulate your spouse to get your way; using "bargaining chips" to "buy" what you want from your spouse; a win-or-lose attitude.

VIRTUE: COOPERATION/INSPIRATION

Manifested as the ability to balance your own and your spouse's needs and desires; a win-win orientation to conflict resolution; a sense of security and trust in the relationship that enables you to "give in" to your spouse without the sense that you have been taken advantage of.

CHECKLIST

1. You coerced your spouse into giving in to you by nagging, bugging, or irritating him or her.

2. You successfully worked out a disagreement on a practical matter by negotiating a solution that both of you felt good about.

3. You "blew up" at your spouse over a small matter.

4. You forgave your spouse freely and completely, without demands or conditions.

5. You held a grudge against your spouse for something he or she did. You were not open to talking to him or her about it for a long time.

6. You were able to "give in" on a key point in a problem area. You did not feel that you had been taken advantage of, but rather you felt positive about your action.

7. You have demanded a particular concession or action from your spouse repeatedly, even though it is clear that he or she is not prepared to do it at this time.

8. You clearly and assertively expressed your feeling, desire, or need to your spouse in an area that has been a sensitive and anxiety-provoking topic for you.

9. You have set expectations for your spouse that you yourself do not fulfill.

10. You have given up a long-standing resentment toward your spouse, and you view it as a positive move for yourself and the relationship.

Need Value: Economic Well-being

Of all the things couples will argue about, money tops the list. Not that money is so important, but it is often the means to obtaining particular goals. It is also tied to an individual's sense of control and security over personal well-being.

DEFECT: WASTEFULNESS/POVERTY

Manifested as a tendency to spend money unwisely; shopping or spending money compulsively; misusing family funds on selfish pursuits; impulsive decision making regarding investments and finances; excessive frugality; greed.

VIRTUE: PRODUCTIVITY/RESOURCEFULNESS

Manifested as the ability to economize, maximize resources, and spend money wisely; generosity; willingness to invest time, energy, and money for the family's long-term benefit; productivity.

CHECKLIST

1. You purchased an item for yourself without considering if other members of your family may need or want something and have to do without.

2. You saved money by spending your time and effort to find a bargain.

3. You spent money on credit above your family's ability to pay.

4. You and your spouse jointly set a financial goal and achieved it (such as saving toward a down payment on a house).

5. You hid sales receipts or bills from your spouse because you feared his or her reaction.

6. You trusted your spouse completely to spend money wisely while shopping for the family, gifts, and so forth.

7. You had the means to provide for a need or desire of your spouse or other family member, but you found it hard to let go of the money.

8. You and your spouse agreed on a specific plan for your retirement or long-range financial well-being.

9. You spent money set aside for a specific purpose (such as retirement, savings, or the college fund) for a consumer item that you wanted without your spouse's agreement.

10. You bought a substantial item for your spouse or your family without wanting something in return.

Need Value: Personal Well-being

There are effective ways of responding to life's stresses and ineffective ways. Ridding yourself of emotional baggage carried over from the past, changing aspects of your surroundings, and taking decisive action can reinforce your personal sense of security or well-being.

DEFECT: IRRITABILITY/ANXIETY

Manifested as a tendency to worry, become anxious, or fearful about problems; pessimism; emotional dependency on your spouse; lack of independence; depression, unhappiness, gloom about your life, marriage, family, or life situation.

VIRTUE: SATISFACTION/HAPPINESS

Manifested as the ability to face challenges with optimism; skill in releasing anxiety and fear; enjoyment of life's pleasures; ability to view life from a positive rather than negative perspective; ownership of your problems and the ability to plan.

CHECKLIST

1. You were in a gloomy or bad mood, and it negatively affected your spouse.

2. You and your spouse planned and enjoyed a short trip or vacation.

3. You experienced fears and anxiety about some activities or situations that are not uncommon (such as going to social gatherings, driving to unfamiliar or busy areas, being alone at night).

4. You planned and did an activity that you enjoyed for yourself and by yourself.

5. You assumed the worst about your spouse or other family member but found out you were mistaken.

6. You "snapped out" of a gloomy or depressed mood by doing something productive or enjoyable.

7. You felt unable to handle a problem without your spouse.

8. You felt a sense of joy and contentment with your life.

9. You worried about your spouse, a family member, or a situation but did not really do anything to help.

10. You felt inspired and positive about life and did something positive, inspiring, or spontaneous toward your spouse as a result.

Need Value: Responsibility

Responsibility flows from the interconnectedness of human lives. Human needs and desires are very interdependent. Responsibility brings respectability since you make a contribution to the general welfare.

DEFECT: SELFISHNESS/UNFAITHFULNESS

Manifested as a tendency to put yourself ahead of others; self-centeredness; inability to empathize and see your spouse's point of view; irresponsibility; planning or manipulating to avoid work; sexual infidelity.

VIRTUE: AUTHENTICITY/COMMITMENT

Manifested by consideration of your spouse's needs and desires; willingness to put work and energy into your relationship and life together; an explicit and spiritual commitment to stay with your spouse; integrity; fidelity.

CHECKLIST

1. You insisted your spouse do an activity that you wanted to do rather than what he or she wanted.

2. You spontaneously did something that you knew your spouse wanted you to do, without being asked first.

3. You "dumped" a problem on your spouse without really offering help.

4. You formed a plan of action to deal with a family problem and carried out your plan. You handled the problem on your own.

5. You expected your spouse to handle a major problem by himself or herself.

6. You put aside an enjoyable or recreational activity to help your spouse with something that is important to him or her.

7. You were sexually unfaithful.

8. You allowed your spouse or other family member to be the center of attention and enjoyed watching it.

9. You abandoned your responsibility, and your family suffered as a result.

10. On your own initiative, you identified an ongoing area of need for the family and made a plan to fulfill it.

Need Value: Sexual Fulfillment

This may be awkward to talk about with your partner, but try to be completely honest. So many misunderstandings can be cleared up by facing the issues with forthrightness.

DEFECT: ALIENATION/SELF-ABSORPTION

Manifested as the tendency to be wrapped up in your own sexual wants and needs to the exclusion of your partner's; inability to focus your sexuality on your marriage relationship; boredom; unwillingness to believe that your sexual relationship with your spouse can improve; repeated sexual infidelity; impotence, lack of desire, or "frigidity"; unwillingness to change and learn; frustration.

VIRTUE: ENJOYMENT/INTEGRATION

Manifested by the ability to enjoy your spouse sexually; contentment and satisfaction with your sex life; attentiveness to your spouse's sexual wants and needs; willingness to learn, change, and grow; excitement; intimacy.

CHECKLIST

1. You demanded or wanted to demand something of your spouse in your sexual relationship.

2. You felt especially happy and content in making love to your spouse.

3. You have given up hope that your sexual relationship with your spouse can improve.

4. You tried something new sexually with your spouse.

5. You had secret lust for someone other than your spouse.

6. You planned a romantic interlude with your spouse.

7. You secretly admired or envied an acquaintance who indulges in promiscuity.

8. You discussed a sexual problem with your spouse; he or she listened and you found a solution together.

9. You have experienced impotence, "frigidity," lack of desire, or other sexual dysfunctions and have not sought help.

10. You did something for your spouse sexually that you know is especially exciting to him or her.

Need Value: Parenting

Children are often the dumping ground for troubles between parents. You cannot completely avoid making mistakes, but they can be minimized through a cooperative partnership between mother and father.

DEFECT: ABUSIVENESS/INEFFECTIVENESS

Manifested as the tendency to verbally abuse children, including demeaning, disrespectful, or cruel speech; neglecting to give attention and energy needed to provide structure and direction for children; ineffective discipline; alienation or disaffection from your children; disagreement with your spouse about parenting.

VIRTUE: NURTURANCE/EFFECTIVENESS

Manifested as the ability to provide nurturance, protection, and a caring environment for children; effective discipline; enjoyment of activities with children; agreement with your spouse on parenting issues.

CHECKLIST

1. You angrily chided your son or daughter and said things that you regretted later.

2. You handled a parenting challenge by yourself, without having to "call in" your spouse.

3. You put off your child's want or need in favor of your own less important want or need.

4. You analyzed a recurring behavioral problem, talked about it with your spouse, and came up with a unified and effective strategy for dealing with it.

5. You realized that your child goes to your spouse for fulfillment of his or her need for affection because you have not been as positive and affectionate as you can be with him or her.

6. You enjoyed an activity with your child.

7. You argued with your spouse over the kids or over an important parenting issue.

8. You and your spouse successfully backed each other up when your child tried to split your opinion over a particular issue.

9. You felt despair that your child's behavior will ever improve in a particular area.

10. You felt that you trust and respect your spouse's ability as a parent.

5

CONFESSION

STEP FIVE: ADMITTED TO GOD, TO OURSELVES,
AND TO ANOTHER HUMAN BEING THE EXACT NA-
TURE OF OUR WRONGS.

*His was "Geepers" and hers was "Gordita" ("Little
Plump One"). Not really romantic nicknames, that was simply what they called each other privately. No one else even
knew of these names. Not that they kept them a secret; it
just seemed inappropriate to refer to their spouse by these
names except between each other. If they were separated in
a crowded supermarket or calling to each other above the
noise of traffic, they could always make out the sound of
these names in what amounted to their own unique form of
a love call.*

*"Gordita" was more than a name. Even though at vari-
ous times in her life she thought it an apt description of
herself—especially after the birth of their first child—she
knew that whenever Geepers called her by that name he
was conveying much more to her. She did not remember
when in their fourteen years of marriage he had begun calling her Gordita. She only remembered feeling very special
each time he did. When he was away on business and
would telephone, she felt him nearer whenever she picked
up the telephone and heard him say, "Hello, Gordita."*

*"Geepers" came sort of by accident. As a small child,
when he was upset, instead of crying he would hold his*

breath and, like a rocket taking off, this low grumble would slowly rise out of him and he would shout "Oh Geepers!" Like all nicknames, somehow it just stuck.

As married couples do, they had found a password which gave access to one another's soul. These names were not only a form of identification between themselves, they conveyed how they felt about each other. They defined the word love as it applied to them. They expressed how inextricably linked their lives were. These names were charged with all the passion of their struggles, their fights, and of every time they had ever made love together—all rolled into one word.

"What's in a name?" Shakespeare wrote, "That which we call a rose, by any other name would smell as sweet." Step Five is all about naming the reality of who you both are as a result of your history and as a result of the freedom of choice which is yours right now.

Step Five works off the increased awareness of the Step Four Moral Inventory. It asks that you, in an unbiased, nonjudgmental way declare to yourself, to God, and to one other human being, "This is who I am." For better or worse, through good times and bad, you make a deliberate act of self-acceptance. Self-acceptance is the doorway to understanding and acceptance of your spouse. Like the nicknames given between lovers, this step is taken with great reverence and tenderness toward yourself and shared with only a privileged few.

Rarely can we see deeply into our own souls. A person is biased toward his or her own point of view. Perspective is hard to retain. It is a struggle to identify precisely what the heart of the problem is, but this is the main task. To be sidetracked on secondary issues leads nowhere. To name the demon that haunts you and call it out of yourself is a formidable task. Marital problems can be like a lot of tangled ropes that ensnare related and unrelated issues. Once named, however, you have gained a foothold in conquering the problems.

There are two sides to the word *confess*. You might confess your guilt, in the sense of admitting to doing something wrong. But you might also confess in the sense of stating your belief in something. "I confess that I love you," for example. Step Five is the action that distinguishes between the defect of character and you the person. To take Step Five is not only to divulge what you have done wrong, but to affirm your belief in your value as a person. For you to explain to someone, for example, that you have had an affair for which you are sorry, says something about how important fidelity is to you. The character defect is always set in the context of the character strength. The spot on the proverbial apple stands out because the major portion of the apple is still good.

Just because you have broken a rule that you value does not mean you no longer hold that value. Remember, defects of character are instincts misdirected toward the fulfillment of needs you have as a human being. Even though you went about satisfying a need in an ineffective way, the need persists. This is the part of you that must be accepted and affirmed. Perhaps you engaged in an extramarital affair to meet a need for intimacy. Just because you broke off the affair does not mean the need for intimacy has been fulfilled. Stating this fact explicitly means accepting that need for intimacy within you.

THE EXACT NATURE OF OUR WRONGS

Step Five focuses your healing powers where they are needed. To identify this or that particular action as harmful to another or to yourself also affirms the desire for a more effective solution. To name the exact nature of your wrongs is to discover their origins, and therefore, the exact nature of your culpability or responsibility.

For example, sometimes emotions are mislabeled. What you may be calling "guilt" over something you did may in fact be sadness at having taken actions that upset someone else. You are responsible for the action you took. The reaction is the other person's responsibility. For example, if a husband says, "I told my wife I didn't like her new haircut and boy did she get mad," he is responsible for the manner in which he states his opinion. He should be sensitive to his wife's reaction to what he says. But it is her responsibility if she feels disappointed, and reacts by getting angry, saying something obscene, and stomping out of the room.

Naming the precise nature of the wrong wins back some of the emotion, self-esteem, and energy expended or misdirected by this mental and emotional entanglement. Some people find, when they first begin to detach themselves from another's responsibility and take their own proper portion, arguments become slightly more emotionally charged. But as they become more focused, the energy of emotion is released faster and therefore the pressure subsides more quickly. It is bottling up that energy that sets up such a blast when the top finally comes off.

Remorse for the wrongs you have done is a healthy sign. Remorse alone, however, does not alter the situation or change behavior. No doubt you or your spouse have made promises to each other that you simply did not or could not keep. Willpower alone will not make it happen. Acceptance of the underlying needs within you that are not being met is what brings transformation. If the needs will not go away and the manner in which you have sought to fulfill them is causing you and others harm, devising a more enlightened, reasonable plan for dealing with your needs is the answer.

Identifying or naming that particular defect of character in a precise way is in fact the exercise of the virtue of humility. Humility is that quality that enables you to see yourself as you really are with no exaggeration. Humility means you strive to see yourself as no more but no less than you actually are.

Typically in conflict situations, the narrow thinking of the false self is inclined to take all or none of the blame for something. It wants to dramatize the severity of problems and the emotions that go along with them. The compulsive thinker will sometimes acknowledge a degree of responsibility but remain vague about the precise nature of the responsibility, thus evading accountability and the truth, for example, saying, "Yeah, so I screwed up. Big deal."

Some couples fight as though they were shoppers haggling over the price of something. "I know I'm not perfect, but what he did to me is absolutely inexcusable!" The speaker here equates her faults with common human frailty. Her partner, however, is in her opinion extraordinarily blameworthy. One tries to raise the level of responsibility ("absolutely inexcusable"), while the other fights to lower it. These sorts of conflicts require a further step in order to accurately assess who is accountable for what.

One very practical way of exercising humility in your marriage is by integrating the *100 Percent Responsibility Rule*[1] into all of your relations with your spouse. The rule is simply this: "Take 100 percent of your own responsibility; take none of anyone else's."

Responsibility may be best explained by imagining an old-fashioned pinball machine.[2] There are many elements in life over which you have little or no control, such as physical appearance, native intelligence, the family you are born into, your race, and so on. These are aspects of your character you are thrown into life with at birth. These are the "bumpers," the fixed parts of the game that do not change. Matters in which you can exercise some free will may be thought of as the "flippers." You are free to exercise control over these parts of your life, such as your thoughts, perceptions, desires, and actions. Although they may seem small and insignificant, they can make all the difference in the outcome of your experiences. Success in life is all in how skillfully you play the game.

Detachment from that which is beyond your control is the all-important attitude that differentiates between what you are responsible for and what you are not, what you have the power to control and what you do not. Likewise, detachment maintains the line between care or concern for what another person has done and "butting in."

At first, detachment may sound insensitive. Detachment is not indifference. It requires a real commitment to yourself and to the person involved. Accepting full responsibility for yourself implies you will act to the best of your ability in any given situation and refrain from controlling the other person's decisions, emotions, or actions. It actually frees you to give yourself more effectively, and therefore, more lovingly in relationships.

Bob and Laura, whom you met in Chapter One, are a couple in their mid to late forties. They had three children, two girls and a boy. Their son was tragically killed at sixteen in an auto accident, in which he was at fault. Together, Bob and Laura run a family business.

Laura began seeing a counselor, complaining of long-standing depression and anxiety over her marriage. She experienced crying spells about two or three times a week, frequent thoughts of hopelessness, and utter frustration with her husband. Other therapists had suggested that she simply leave her husband, that he was just too difficult to live with. Laura, however, could not justify this within herself. She wanted to do her utmost to make her marriage succeed.

Bob was a troubled man. He had grown up with an alcoholic father and had inherited his irritable disposition. Laura could recount many tales of Bob's explosive temper. He would erupt at the slightest provocation, casting hurtful accusations and insults at her. Bob harbored guilt and took responsibility for his son's death. He, after all, agreed to let his son buy the sports car in which he was killed. In addition, Bob had had several short-term affairs. Laura knew of them and ignored them at first. Later, she felt hurt and resentful toward Bob. When she confronted him about them once he coldly stated, "That's just the way I am." He agreed, however, to break off the affairs.

Laura thought constantly of the day when she would discover Bob had resumed his infidelities and she would be forced to back up her threats to leave him, and actually make the break. It was not what she wanted to happen, but she thought it was inevitable. And so, she lived each day with anxiety, uncertainty, and loneliness.

In counseling for her depression, her therapist suggested she employ the One Hundred Percent Responsibility Rule as a way of counteracting some of the anxiety and stress. Instead of seeing herself as simply a leaf caught in a storm, subject to forces beyond her control, she began to see herself as a person who was battling a storm.

As she began to restructure the way she thought about her predicament, she began to see more and more options open to her. Her task was clear: she would have to decide under what conditions she would remain with Bob. Previously, she had anxiously thought what if this happened, what if that happened. Now, she was working out a sequence of possible situations and her responses. In this way she felt in charge of her own life, instead of reacting to Bob all the time.

The first decision was what she would do if indeed Bob became involved in another extramarital affair. After much soul searching, she decided she would probably leave him. She would, however, not be able to really decide until it happened. So, until that time, she would stop telling herself, "I am going to have to leave Bob," as though it were inevitable.

Laura reflected on her marriage and accepted a certain amount of responsibility for the conflicts. However, she also refused to take responsibility for Bob's actions. As the old saying goes, "It takes two to tango." Laura did her best not to dance. When Bob launched into a tirade over a certain chair he had wanted in a certain place, but which Laura had removed from its usual spot, Laura allowed Bob to fume and rage without saying to herself, "I am responsible for his being angry."

This was what was causing her depression. He would bark and yell and she would take it all very calmly, or so she thought. But then she would be depressed for the next three days. On this occasion, however, she launched right back at him. "You can't be serious!" she said. "Do you expect me to be a mind reader and know what you want twenty-four hours a day?"

As she thought about it later, she took responsibility for her anger. She had been hooked into a futile struggle of words and putdowns. She replayed the scene in her mind thinking about what she should have said.

"Yes," she could have said to Bob, "I could have consulted

with you before I rearranged the room. That would have been better."

The issue was not finished just by Laura acknowledging her mistake. She also refused to take responsibility for Bob's abusive outburst. She thought about it to herself and expressed to Bob her displeasure at his yelling and assertively asked him to find another way of communicating his disagreement. She took all of her own responsibility, but refused to accept what was properly Bob's responsibility.

Of course, Bob's uncontrolled rage was inappropriate. This was something he was responsible for, not Laura. She had to take care not to let her own insecurities or depressed state play into his dysfunctions. She had to take care of her health and he was responsible for his.

Progress was slow in coming. Every time Laura was able to detach herself from Bob's responsibilities, there seemed to be two more occasions when she clicked into her old habits. After about three months of diligent "responsibility taking," careful self-examination, and prayer over her behavior toward Bob, however, Laura began to see a positive change in her mood. She began to believe that she was powerless to change Bob directly, but not powerless to change her attitude toward the things she was powerless over. She began to accept the fixed parts of her life, the things she could not change, and to exercise her freedom in the areas she could.

Laura recognized that responsibility for her life entailed not only the mistakes she made, but also the things she did right, the things at which she was good and successful. She realized responsibility for herself involved treating herself fairly and respectfully, and to recognize when she was just too tired to deal with problems effectively and should wait for a better time.

TO GOD, TO OURSELVES, AND TO ANOTHER HUMAN BEING

Some people will ask, "Why is Step Five so important?" Recalling and relating the wounded areas of your life to another person calls out of you deep feelings from within your heart. Initial feelings of fear or sadness at recounting to another your misdeeds may inhibit you. But these will give way to deeper, stronger urgings from your truer inner self. As the whole immune system reacts to expel disease from the body, so your whole being reacts to expel what threatens your life as a whole; the body wants to be healthy, the soul struggles for wholeness.

The solution to many of your problems lies within you. The solutions are within you as well as without. You are not dependent upon a particular person or miracle chemical to supply the cure. The insanity of obsessive thinking is that it sets you up to think that everything good, valuable, loving, or meaningful is outside of you. Consequently, you must earn, pay for, or depend on someone else for all these things. The truth is, the solution comes from something you already possess. The strength to make Step Five comes from that fundamental belief in the power of your own person.

Strong feelings can lie beneath the surface of your demeanor, so that when you try to speak about even a loosely related topic, the feelings well up uncontrollably. For example, you may become teary eyed when you hear a certain song or feel tension when someone touches you. These are just some indications that issues are continuing to affect you because of a failure to effectively deal with them.

Your body and your psyche tend toward health. The energy of emotions craves release. Like water rushing downhill, when there are no obstacles, the healing process will proceed quicker than you imagine to the heart of the matter. Step Five clears your conscience and uncovers the distortion caused by obsessive thinking. As difficult and emotionally stirring as Step Five may be for you initially, it eventually brings greater awareness and experience of your deeper, truer self. In taking Step Five there must be an explicit act of self-acceptance. Denial or self-deception is cleared away. The emotions of guilt and shame are released and you are put in touch, again, with your own power.

Admitting the true nature of your wrongs to God opens you to receive the acceptance of God, the firm foundation of your life.

This can be a struggle since it implies you have a relationship with God that is trusting enough to accept any judgment that comes from God. Recall that your Higher Power is your ally. Anything you withhold only separates you from His power to aide you. Being anything less than completely honest keeps you isolated from others.

Do not presume the person to whom you make this confession will be, or should be, your spouse. It would be safe to assume that a level of complete and unconditional acceptance toward one another is not yet present. This is not to say it cannot be someday. Indeed, this is your goal. But for now, consider someone else in whom you have complete confidence: your sponsor, a trusted friend, a therapist, a clergyperson, anyone before whom you will not fail to reveal your true self.

How important is this third part to Step Five? It is vital! It is vital that the true self inside of you become the basis from which you relate to yourself, to God, to your spouse, and every human being. It is vital for your continued recovery that the true self, which has no doubt been misjudged and maltreated, be at some time affirmed and encouraged. It is not enough to keep secrets between you and God. This part of Step Five is the action by which you complete the return from isolation, from the world of your own making to the world of reality. It makes acceptance of your humanity real by receiving the unconditional acceptance of another.

It is important to note that the experience of acceptance may not come in the exact order presented here. Often real self-acceptance does not come until we have received the loving affirmation of another. Sometimes a person is willing to fully admit his or her mistakes to God only after hearing the perspective of a friend. The companionship of whomever you choose will give you courage.

It is normal to experience some fearfulness. This is the signal that you are being honest. Anyone can talk calmly about things that are of little consequence. It is when you feel deeply about something that you have trouble finding the words to express what you feel and become wary of just who to confide in. Allow yourself to share that important matter with another person, and let that sharing draw you out of isolation. This sharing may lead you to tears. Let it happen. It is not an impression you are trying to leave with anyone; it is a bit of the real you. How often have you wanted to express some of these thoughts and feelings to someone and not had the opportunity? Now is your chance.

Some people discover after taking Step Five that they have forgotten something. As you become more enlightened about your own situation, an event in your history may take on a new and different meaning. It is okay to go back to that person with whom you made Step Five and add to it. Likewise, subsequent wrongs to someone ought to be faced with the same degree of openness and honesty. Keep in mind, the goal of recovery is to free yourself from those character defects that inhibit the fulfillment of your human needs. Your marriage is something that must serve those needs for both of you.

THANK YOU, THANK YOU

When Evelyn heard the door click shut behind her she stopped. She had just bid her sponsor a cheery good-bye and confidently turned to leave. At the instant that she knew she was finally alone, she paused on the porch and looked out. A roar of applause went up in front of her, a standing ovation inside her head as the sound of the leaves rustling in the trees greeted her ears. She smiled and humbly accepted congratulations, murmuring quietly but audibly, "Thank you, thank you."

The trees continued to congratulate her as she passed beneath them on the way to her car. She had just finished making Step Five, an event she could never have conceived of undergoing six months ago. Now that it was over, she could only feel that she had completed an extraordinary phase of her life and was beginning a new one now.

Two years ago, Evelyn had left her husband, Oscar. Left him forever, she thought. But after a nearly two-year separation, in which they could neither stay together nor stay apart, they both had grown to where they wanted to try to pull it together again. Evelyn cautiously began applying the Twelve Steps to her marriage, making her own growth and happiness the ultimate goal. If it brought Oscar and her back together, great. If not, at least the two of them would be on the road to their respective destinies.

As she began her work, she recognized fear played a tremendous part in her decisions, attitudes, and relations with others. Her spiritual resolve was to do whatever would lead to her own personal well-being, whether she liked it or not. Come what may, she wanted her life to move forward. Evelyn would not let her own fears turn her around.

It was the specificity of Steps Four and Five that made her nervous, having to pin down the exact nature of her wrorgs. It was painful for her to think about her own part in the breakdown of their relationship. It was painful to feel the feelings of many years, sometimes going back to her childhood. But feeling it again was part of the cure—she knew this deep inside. Having the courage to persevere was what she prayed for, what she trusted her Higher Power to provide.

It was a complex of issues that made her dread Step Five in particular. The fact that she left Oscar buried her in guilt and shame. At the time she felt justified. He had been working himself into a frenzy, losing all sense of perspective. She felt he had little or no romantic interest in her and was becoming more and more of a tyrant toward their four children. She was lonely and frustrated.

She kept telling Oscar she thought that he didn't love her anymore and she wasn't sure if she loved him. This upset Oscar, who would then explode in anger. He would insist that he did love her but that she was impossible to talk to. "She would pout and mope," he said. As time went by, and as Evelyn became more and more depressed, she saw only one solution.

A girlfriend Evelyn had been sharing her frustrations with suggested she and Oscar separate. She needed a roommate and

Evelyn would be welcome to stay with her as long as she needed or wanted to. Without much fanfare or explanation, Evelyn moved out of her home and in with her friend. She just needed time to think, she told Oscar.

Evelyn had been facing a kind of relational "meltdown" in her life. She hadn't the energy for anyone. Much of her life she had acted as the "caretaker" of the family. As a child, she worked harder than all the other children to help around the house. It was to her that her sisters would come for comfort and advice. She cared about people deeply. Even in her marriage, she worried about what Oscar was thinking. Fearful and seldom spontaneous with her feelings, she simply appeared shy to most people. In her own mind, she felt burdened.

The time apart was good for her. It helped her to recognize her need to strengthen herself from within. When she focused her attention on discovering a satisfaction within herself, feeling confident and able to reach for what she needed, she began to feel free enough to let others get close to her.

In her moral inventory, Evelyn focused on her own self-esteem and her desire for security. She saw these as the key issues. She wanted Oscar to be strong and decisive, and yet she grew depressed because he seemed to be uncaring toward her feelings.

Evelyn acknowledged her own timidity kept her at a distance from Oscar. She did not like to fight. She wasn't good at it. She couldn't remember things she wanted to say to him when she was speaking to him. She became nervous and embarrassed. As she began to take charge of her own life, taking responsibility for her own well-being and happiness, she recognized she would still have to take some risks if she was going to experience the intimacy she wanted.

In reviewing her own role in the breakup of her marriage, Evelyn thought about the unfair things she had said to Oscar, the gossip she had spread about him. She also recognized that her reluctance to confront him on matters led to hurt feelings and misunderstandings. Her own insecurity made her somewhat passive in articulating her wants and needs. She would have to learn to speak up for herself. Thus, in her inventory she focused on her need for a greater sense of personal well-being and security and satisfying that need constructively.

She examined her life and relationships for the origins of this character defect. She tried to recall incidents where her own personal fears and insecurities made her anxious, curt, hyper-vigilant, and so forth. She recognized patterns going back to her childhood. Her father had been a loud, boisterous man who dominated the family with his personality. Evelyn sincerely believed he loved his wife and children, but from a very young age she feared him. He was tall and broad, with a strong voice and stern face.

Her mother was a strong woman as well, but in an unmistakably feminine way. She was a dutiful wife who rode above the roar of her husband's voice. To Evelyn, her mother was governed by an invisible line that if crossed by her father would prompt direct and forceful reaction. Everything else she tuned out. She was his anchor, keeping him balanced.

Taken together, Evelyn acknowledged strong feelings of abandonment. On important occasions in her life (such as when she succeeded at something or, more importantly, when she experienced failure or disappointment) where she desired affection, recognition, or affirmation, she felt embarrassed to seek it out from her mother and afraid to appear weak in front of her father. There were times as a little girl she worried about being separated from her parents and then getting left behind somewhere.

Oscar, her husband, was also a strong, direct sort of fellow. When he was angry everybody knew it. In truth though, Evelyn detected a definite difference in his anger and her father's. Oscar's anger, although overt, was not directed toward anyone in particular. He let off steam. He blew his stack like a steam boat. But nobody, other than himself, seemed to be affected. He did not shout insults at her or make threats. He just sort of rushed around the room huffing and puffing, waving his arms and shouting his side of the story. It was like watching him in fast motion with the volume turned up.

The problem, as Evelyn saw it, was her own conditioned response to angry voices and hot tempers. She could not detach herself from Oscar's emotions as her mother once did with her father's. She could not detect that invisible line of responsibility. Consequently, she was not only afraid of Oscar's emotions, she was also afraid of her own emotions and what they might cause Oscar to feel. She was caught in a vicious circle.

This was what she perceived as the heart of her mismatch with Oscar. She overwhelmed herself with the emotions of others—real or imagined. Life with her father had made her highly sensitive to what everyone else was thinking and feeling. She had learned to set her own emotions, and therefore her own self-worth, aside to accommodate her father's unruly ways.

This was where she felt she had to take responsibility for some of the problems in her relationship with Oscar. Her character defect of low self-esteem, conditioned by an upbringing which did not meet her need for affection and affirmation, led her to a pattern of relating that basically said, "If I can display only pleasing emotions and say pleasant things, Oscar (you can substitute "father") will be happy and then I will get the loving attention I desire." This formed the core defect of her confession.

Once she named the basic defect accurately, she grew in understanding of it by what she read and what she shared with other people. This helped her to feel compassion for herself. Step Five, Evelyn recognized, was the next logical step.

Pressing forward, she could not stop now. She would take Step Five because it was the action needed to confirm the thought. Her fears would continue to consume her resolve until she acted against them. If she really meant what she was telling herself, then she would have to demonstrate it in a tangible way.

As she tried to pull these thoughts together, it was suggested that she follow a basic format. First, she had to be specific about the behavior for which she was accountable and how it affected someone else; for example, "I have said things to Oscar that were either not true or were not the whole truth. As a result, he was intentionally misled into believing something that was not so."

Secondly, she had to identify the basic need the behavior was trying to fulfill. In this case, she was attempting to secure his expressions of affection and esteem for her. This desire had to be consciously acknowledged as a legitimate human need. She was to embrace her humanity, not degrade or deny it. The affection she craved was not being possessive or selfish. It is an authentic need! She had to recognize the destructive voices that mislabeled things in order to control her.

Thirdly, feelings of guilt or shame had to be identified. She had to understand where they came from. Did the feeling relate to real responsibility or not? And finally, in formulating what she did wrong, she was to accept it fully as a part of her history, taking care to foster a compassion for that wounded part of her humanity.

Writing this out in her journal, she realized much of the work of acceptance had already taken place. Detachment had naturally begun to occur as she sorted the events out in her mind. Evelyn felt she was growing in strength with the completion of each part of her preparation.

Admission to God of who she was brought about a tremendous transformation in her relationship with God. God had always been someone she tried to please, like her father or mother. "Doing good, this is what brings God close to you," she would say to herself. In taking Step Five, she began to experience God standing beside her whether she was able to do good or not. God was someone who had joined her side in a struggle against something within her that was stifling her.

Because Evelyn was not worried about attaching blame or justification to her wrongs, she felt free to empathize at times with her mistakes, even though looking back she saw the folly of her thinking. She felt vindicated in a certain respect. This made telling her story to someone else not only easier but more necessary. She had to tell her story to someone. She had to make someone understand.

A lifetime of being out of touch with her own goodness, not having had that reflected back to her as a child in the affirmation of her parents, made sharing her story with another human being essential. Intellectually she could see what was missing in her background. Yet, she was too afraid to explain it to her husband. Even if she tried, not having actually had a recognizable experience of it, she would be unable to clearly express what she was asking for. She needed to have an experience of what she was missing before she would be able to describe it and actively seek it. Taking Step Five and sharing herself completely with another human being would give her that experience.

"The experience of working Step Five left me emptied. It was a great experience of human kindness. I felt freed from a lot of guilt. But walking away from it I felt a lightness that made me uncomfortable. For so much of my life I had been bound to this person or tied to that one, after taking that fifth step, I felt like I wanted to wrap myself up in a blanket, to cover myself again. But I resisted. I knew this was the freedom that eluded me in relationships. Now I had the sense that I was choosing to be part of my marriage, as well as any other relationship. I was free. I was in charge of my life.

"One day, after I had taken Step Five, Oscar called. We had been hinting around about getting back together. As we talked I noticed that feeling of lightness was with me again. I felt at ease as we spoke. I felt at peace with the way I was handling myself. We talked more freely than we ever had when we were together. I felt differently about myself and that had an influence on the way I reacted toward the things he said. It influenced the things I chose to say to him, and the way I said them.

"I felt like the prospects of our getting back together had improved. I felt I was really opening myself up to Oscar, and at the same time, I was not in fear of losing something. I was not afraid that he possessed a part of me that I had to beg him to give back to me.

"At the end of the conversation, I thanked him for calling. I told him how special it had been to be able to talk freely and honestly. I said I was encouraged about the way our relationship was improving. I said it really warmed my heart to know he understood me, my points of view, and even some sides of my personality that I was only beginning to discover, but that he had been all too painfully introduced to. A familiar feeling of security flashed through me, I told him, when I picked up the phone and heard that familiar voice say, "Hello, Gordita."

STEP GUIDE: STEP FIVE

Step Five should be written out. Don't rely on your memory for it all. Also, setting it down in black and white helps you to be more precise about the exactness of the wrong. Remember, there is no virtue in distorting the facts one way or the other. Tell it like it is. Use your Step Four Inventory as a starting point.

The following may help you break down the task into meaningful categories.

1. Compose a personal life history.

2. Include incidents that involve your having harmed another in the following categories:

FAMILY: parents (living or deceased), brothers, sisters, spouses and children, in-laws, extended relatives.

EMPLOYMENT: supervisors, co-workers, clients.

ORGANIZATIONS: churches, hospitals, schools.

RELATIONSHIPS WITH OTHERS: friends, strangers, neighbors.

DISTRESSING AND HUMILIATING FACTS: stealing, lying, physical harm, sexual abuse.

3. Using your personal life history, which includes the exact nature of your wrongs, tell your story to another human being.

4. After sharing your story with another person, take some time to be alone. In the solitude reread the Twelve Steps carefully. Consider whether anything has been left out to this point. Recognize you are laying a firm foundation from which to live every day of your life. If you have responded to each question satisfactorily, you will be ready to move on to Step Six.

5. While you are alone you may want to say a prayer of gratitude for having come this far. The following is offered as a suggestion:

Thank You, God, for creating me as I am, just as I am today. No wisdom I could derive could have brought me to this point of wholeness. What I am and will become, with Your loving assistance, I accept and welcome.

Fill me with the power to appreciate the good and beauty around me. Fill me with the wisdom to conduct myself rightly, honestly, truthfully. Guide me through my journey to restore my life to where I can welcome intimacy with my spouse, _____, my family, and all others I am privileged to meet. Amen.

6

READINESS

STEP SIX: WE WERE ENTIRELY READY TO HAVE GOD REMOVE THESE DEFECTS OF CHARACTER.

Congratulations! You have completed the first major house-cleaning task of your Twelve Step work with the completion of Steps Four and Five. You have a solid foundation for working the rest of your program. Progress began with surrender of your spouse and his or her character defects to God. Your acceptance of God's positive will and intent for you and your spouse freed you from the obsession of trying to change your spouse. Instead, you turned to the task of taking a fearless and searching moral inventory of yourself. The inventory gave you insights into the origins of your character defects which disrupt your marriage. In Step Five, you came to a humble acceptance of yourself by acknowledging to God, yourself, and another trustworthy person, the exact nature of your defects of character. These steps have enabled you to take full responsibility for your part in healing your marriage and have made it easier for your spouse to accept his or her responsibility as well.

Now that you have some idea of *how* your character defects work against you and your marriage, it is time to ask *what* you can do about them. How can you go about changing the defects of character that are destructive to you and your marriage? You start by contending with the resentment over past hurts, healing hurtful memories and becoming willing to forgive.

READINESS

How do you become entirely ready? What is "readiness" anyway? The answer lies in the foundation you have been building.

This foundation is your Higher Power, which is able to surmount any and all obstacles. Thus, in becoming ready to have God remove your character defects, you are deciding to let Him do what for you is impossible. In other words, you are applying the One Hundred Percent Responsibility Rule to your relationship with God. Recall that the rule states, "Take all of your responsibility but none of the other person's." Applying this rule in your relationship with God means that you do all that you possibly can to remove your character defects, but you don't try to do yourself what can only be done by God. You want to be rid of your character defects—particularly the ones most hurtful to your spouse. And you want your spouse to be rid of his or her character defects—especially the ones you find most hurtful.

If only you could flip a switch and make it happen with no effort! But that is not the way it works. There is a process that makes it more likely that your spouse will be freed of his or her character defects. You started the process by releasing control of your spouse's failings. The process is completed by you and your spouse taking your own portions of responsibility. Your spouse's work can only be completed by your spouse and God. This growth is more likely now that you have released control. You have already altered the chemistry of your relationship for the better!

In the same way, however, you cannot flip a switch to rid yourself of your own character weaknesses, either. This is how powerless you really are. But does this mean it is hopeless? No. Just as when the alcoholic finally admits he or she is powerless over alcohol the way to recovery is opened, when you admit your powerlessness over your own character defects renewal of your marriage becomes possible.

What is possible for you to do today is to decide to work a

good program for yourself each day, one day at a time, as it relates to your own character defects. When an alcoholic admits his powerlessness over alcohol it does not give him permission to go out and drink as much as he wants. Rather, he decides to abstain from alcohol one day at a time. Since you are powerless over your character defects, you have the power to do the same: decide to work a good program for today. Identify the next small step you must take to make progress on your side of the marriage problem and take that step today. You cannot guarantee tomorrow. So decide to do what you can, one day at a time.

Of course, this is easier said than done. The first and primary obstacle to becoming ready to do this is—you guessed it—your spouse's character defects. More specifically, though, it is your own tendency to focus on his or her character defects which prevents you from taking the next step of dealing with your own.

It is normal at this point for couples in a troubled marriage to experience a setback, to slip into old errors and habits that make matters worse. You may begin to think, "I have given him emotional support when I haven't really felt like it. I have really tried to accept my partner as he is, faults and all. I have stopped obsessing about and complaining about his behavior. But things still aren't any better! In fact, it seems that they may not get better. He's still doing what he always has. Nothing has changed." You may find it the most difficult thing in the world to catch yourself in thoughts like these and consciously shift back to a focus on yourself. Yet, this is your task.

What possible reason could there be for doing what your partner refuses to do? The reason is simple: If you have decided to work a Twelve Step program, this is precisely the next step. Step Six calls for the willingness to give up your most cherished character flaws, even in the event your spouse never decides to give up his or hers. You may always hope and pray that your partner will decide to give up this or that character flaw. You may even decide that you are unable to live with him or her as long as these character defects persist at the same level. Step Six, however, requires your personal willingness to give up your own character defects—because it's good for *you*.

A STEP SIX STORY

Remember Jennifer and Sean from Chapter Four? Their fights started off as constructive interchanges but quickly turned into destructive arguments with name calling, finger pointing, and even hitting.

Jennifer and Sean decided to visit relatives in New York City over the holidays. Jennifer was very excited about the trip and, in spite of the marriage problems she and Sean had been having, she was hopeful that it would be like a second honeymoon—a time to resolve their differences.

Jennifer loved the city in the holiday season—the bright lights, shopping, and crowds. Sean enjoyed these things too, but not as much as Jennifer. One day they decided to go shopping. Jennifer was elated with the atmosphere the city and the season created. It was part of her job to be aware of new clothing styles, and it was a part she very much enjoyed. Sean, on the other hand, was tired by lunchtime. But he went along with Jennifer just the same. Although he did not want to, he knew how much it meant to her, and he was afraid that she would become angry.

He thought, "She'll accuse me of never wanting to do the things she likes, like she always does. . . ."

By the end of the day, Sean was exhausted and terribly frustrated. Jennifer wanted to visit still more shops, but Sean finally said with irritation that he was tired and wanted to go back to the hotel room.

Jennifer was visibly annoyed, but Sean felt that he could not go on. "She knows I dislike this shopping stuff and that I'm doing it for her, and yet she pushes for more!" Sean said. He told Jennifer he would meet her back at the room and left in a cab.

Twenty minutes after he arrived at the room, Jennifer came in steaming mad. "You left me all alone in the middle of New

York! I didn't know where you went. No one I know is as inconsiderate and insensitive as you!"

She was so angry Jennifer started hitting Sean as she yelled at him. Sean grabbed her and held her till she stopped. Sean's rage at her turned to guilt. He had no idea how things had gotten so out of hand.

After the explosion, Jennifer calmed down and explained that she felt abandoned in a strange city. She had not expected him to actually leave as he did. Sean was bewildered because he felt Jennifer's expectation was not made clear to him. He focused on Jennifer's personality trait that he found most difficult to deal with—her tendency to become demanding and dependent on him at the same time. He thought it was entirely unreasonable of her to expect him to know what she wanted in this situation.

THE PREDICTABLE TRAP

Sean had fallen into the trap so common at this stage of recovery. Even after admitting his powerlessness over Jennifer, turning his will over to his Higher Power, and taking a fearless moral inventory, he succumbed to the temptation (and deeply ingrained habit) of focusing on Jennifer's character flaws.

"She's spoiled rotten! She is like a little kid who throws a tantrum when she doesn't get her way. Even her family knows it! She throws a fit if you don't read her mind. I've had it! I just can't do it anymore!"

Yet he also felt guilty. "I should have been able to avoid this, but I just don't know how. I've tried everything, but there's no pleasing her. I tromped around New York with her for hours. She knew it wasn't my thing; it was for her. But not one bit of appreciation. We're right back where we started."

What happened to Sean? Why is it that he felt all his work in the program was for nought? The simple answer is that he changed his focus, by force of habit, back to Jennifer and her problems. As a result he missed the obvious about himself.

The obvious problem to an outside observer is that Sean was operating out of his own character flaw. He lacked appropriate assertiveness in communicating his fatigue. He had allowed himself to become so tired and frustrated that he began to react impulsively. Sean recognized he had a problem with anger, both his and others'. He knew he overcompensated by projecting an easygoing attitude. His pattern of avoiding confrontation was amplified in this situation because on one hand he knew how much the shopping activity meant to Jennifer and that she would probably become angry if he stated his desire to rest after only half a day had passed. On the other hand, he wanted everything to go perfectly so Jennifer would be happy with him.

Upon reflection, Sean realized this sequence of events was a pattern which had occurred over and over since the beginning of the marriage. In fact, his decision to marry Jennifer at the time he did was based in large part on avoiding her wrath. He knew what she would say if he decided to postpone the wedding.

"She would have said, 'You're not going to pull that "I'm afraid of commitment" crap on me! Decide to commit or break up with me.'" So to avoid the confrontation, he gave in. Both he and Jennifer realized later it would have been better if they had waited.

So, although Jennifer's character flaws contributed to the incident, Sean realized his character flaw of lack of assertiveness was also an essential element leading to that particular blow up.

ONE HUNDRED PERCENT RESPONSIBILITY AND YOUR HIGHER POWER

Sean decided to take full responsibility for his character defect. However, he felt more powerless than ever in the face of it. "I didn't even know I was doing it! I thought I was doing well, giving up my own desire in favor of Jennifer's."

This is where Sean's developing awareness of God's role in his situation came into play. He went back to the core idea of Step

One, "I am powerless even to change my own character defects all at once. Even though I know about the problem, I can't change it."

Sean realized there were critical points at which his response to Jennifer took a turn for the better or for the worse. He truly was easygoing most of the time. He could go along with Jennifer's ideas and activities. But sometimes he fooled himself into thinking it was okay when it really was not okay. He resolved to catch himself and truly question himself at such critical points.

He would do this by asking God's help in these situations. Right there on the spot he would pray, "Not my will but Thy will be done." He would also practice rational thinking in his interpretation of actions and things she would say. In resolving to do this, Sean realized that change would not be immediate. He knew that he would not catch each critical point and would eventually blow up again. He prayed that he could become entirely ready for God to remove this defect by doing his part to be aware of the exact nature of his problem. In this case, he had to take more care to monitor his own feelings and mood.

Readiness, as you can see from Sean and Jennifer's story, is an application of the acceptance and surrender steps to your own character defects. After you have ferreted them out through a moral inventory you have to go to work to change what you can and release what you cannot change over to the power of God. Each time you become aware of another character defect, you repeat the same process.

Readiness, then, has three layers: Spiritual Readiness—understood as the willingness to change; Psychological Readiness—as Sean discovered there has to be a keen awareness of how the defect operates in you and in your marriage; Readiness to Act—even though you know you are going to trip up again you resolve to learn from each new attempt.

WILLINGNESS

Spiritual readiness means willingness to change. Sean hit a stone wall in his own recovery. He alone could do no more. He needed help. He felt his own willingness to work on the marriage beginning to ebb. He had been so deeply hurt and had put so much energy into trying to work with Jennifer, but it seemed to get no results. His sense of powerlessness was very real to him.

Slowly, Sean had begun to take back control. As he made himself and his own will the center of his concern he spent more and more of his energy fruitlessly. He had to surrender again.

Sean had to re-release his quest for control. He had been diligently working his program, all the while keeping his eye on Jennifer for signs of improvement. When he did not see any he became discouraged, and consequently, more prone to focus on Jennifer rather than his own progress.

At this point in his Twelve Step work, Sean was reminded by his sponsor that the very reason he was attracted to Jennifer was those traits she drew out of him. She was the well-suited partner who called out of him his need to stand up for himself, to assert himself in appropriate ways, to take responsibility for addressing and fulfilling his own needs. Consciously or unconsciously, Jennifer put him in touch with those areas of his development that still needed work. Because of his history Sean had these gaps, lapses in his maturity that needed work if he was to be truly happy. Their marriage problems were a blessing in disguise.

The control he worked to establish enabled him to avoid those areas where his own weaknesses were most obvious. Confrontation with Jennifer was something he deeply wanted to avoid. Asserting himself made it almost certain that Jennifer would become angry and lash out at him. So he played the easygoing guy, refraining from expressing legitimate needs and wants until he was about to burst. This was the pattern of their marriage. And yet, if the relationship was to survive, he had to learn how to express himself freely and effectively.

Sean also admitted that when he told Jennifer he was angry or hurt he tended to blame her for his feelings. Even though he understood intellectually that she was not responsible for his anger or hurt, he still blamed her. He retained control by retaining resentment. After all, if he let go of his resentment, what defense would he have against her tongue lashing?

The answer Sean found was simply to stand up for himself and not submit to a tongue lashing. But he was hooked into destructive fights again and again. He knew it was not good to continue a fight when it degenerated into a shouting match or an exchange of hurtful barbs, but he did not know how to stop.

Before he could stand up for himself assertively (and not aggressively), before he was indeed ready to give up his character defect, he had to forgive Jennifer for past hurts and offenses. In doing so, each time they got into a fight his built-up anger and resentment for all of the hurt he had ever suffered at Jennifer's hands would not be rekindled and lead to yet another destructive fight.

FORGIVENESS

Why forgive? There is a popular way of thinking that suggests that if you have been too deeply hurt then you must not forgive. If you forgive, they say, you will open yourself to be hurt again. If you forgive you are allowing yourself to be a victim again. If you forgive, you are somehow approving your spouse's offense—giving it your okay. But this way of thinking misunderstands forgiveness in the Twelve Step program.

Forgiveness is not trust. As we have said, you may forgive your partner and yet not trust your partner, particularly in the specific areas where you have been hurt before. These areas include your partner's character defects and your unfulfilled needs. Forgiveness opens the way for trust to be rebuilt. Trust in these hurtful areas must be earned by your partner if you have been hurt deeply. Don't give your trust unless you feel that it has been earned. Otherwise you may set yourself up for more resentment.

Forgiveness is not forgetting. Forgiveness opens the way for healing, but healing can take time. If you call to mind a fresh and deep offense, it hurts. The hurt does not go away immediately. Hopefully your partner will work a Twelve Step program and will make amends for past hurts. But even amends do not make up for deep hurts. The only one who can forgive your partner for offenses against you is you. It is a free choice which cannot be forced even by amends. As your partner cannot force you to forgive, neither can you force your partner to forgive you. You are powerless over each other when it comes to forgiveness. Neither of you has to forgive. It is a free choice.

Forgiveness is release of the emotional and spiritual debt. When the debt is released, your partner is free to make amends of his or her own free will. There is no guarantee that after you have released the debt your partner will want to make amends. It is your partner's affair. Your work in Step Six requires readiness to have God remove your defects of character. An important part of this readiness includes release of the emotional and spiritual debt your partner owes you since your tendency to act out your character defects is rooted in the resentment you still hold against your partner.

Forgiveness is the release of an emotional and spiritual debt.

Forgiveness implies a desire that amends be made for the hurt, but is not a demand or a requirement of amends.

Forgiveness opens the way for healing hurt and building of trust.

Forgiveness is not . . .
    pretending the offense never happened.
    automatic trust.
    saying, "It's okay that you did that."
    saying, "The relationship is unaffected."
    saying, "Amends are not appropriate or needed."
    submitting to abuse of any type.
    opening yourself to being hurt again.

Forgiveness in the Twelve Step program means the cancellation of an emotional or spiritual debt. Jennifer had trespassed
against Sean on more occasions than he could count. She owed
him.

Sean realized however, according to this definition, that by
admitting his powerlessness over Jennifer and her character defects in Step One, he had already begun to release her from her
debt. In recounting the hurtful incidents between Jennifer and
himself in Step Four, so that he could identify his own character
weaknesses, he had forgiven another portion of her debt.

Now, in becoming spiritually ready to have God remove his
own defects, Sean found it necessary to completely cancel the
debt he held against Jennifer. Although it could be said Jennifer
legitimately owed amends to Sean, he decided to forgive the
debt and require no repayment.

Did this mean Sean had no expectations of Jennifer as his
wife? No. Sean had legitimate expectations and desires of Jennifer, including the important expectation that she not verbally
abuse or nag him. But he canceled the debt for all the times in
the past she had verbally berated him. At the same time, he
decided not to submit to any more.

To become entirely ready to have God remove his character
defects, Sean had to be convinced the defect or control was no
longer needed, that it no longer served his best interests to hold
on to it. This required still further trust in God and in himself.
This releasing of emotional and spiritual debts took him back to
his Step Four Inventory and a review of all the debts he felt
people owed him.

HEALTHY SHAME AND TOXIC SHAME

The resentment Sean felt stemmed from a basic belief that
Jennifer owed him something. It was the same belief he held
about his father. Basically the belief was that if he behaved in a
way that met their expectations, he could expect their love in
return. When his father, and later Jennifer, withheld their love,

they were failing to live up to their part of the bargain, as he understood it. Coupled with Sean's own low self-esteem, the following no-win equation became a core belief in Sean's mind: "The ones I love are withholding their love from me. I love them so much I can't believe they would do it intentionally. Therefore, they must be withholding their love because I have done something wrong."

In Sean's situation the core belief consists of *toxic shame*, which was the result of Sean's experiences at the hands of his alcoholic father. Toxic shame developed as Sean began to believe he was unworthy of love. We saw the development of this belief in Chapter Four. *Healthy shame* never really developed in Sean.

Healthy shame may seem a contradiction in terms, but shame or guilt may be quite healthy when a child realizes, first, he or she is loved and is worthy of love, and second, he or she did something which needs correction.

To overcome the power of the core belief which kept his toxic shame powerfully active in his life, Sean made a decision to turn his will and this area of his life over to the care of God. Sean repeated the process he went through in Step Four. This time he asked his Higher Power to provide the love those close to him were unable to provide. In this way he asked God to do what seemed impossible, namely, to make him truly ready to release his character defects.

Beliefs, memories, and feelings are closely connected. As he considered the presence or absence of love in his life, a flood of memories came to Sean. He revisited the memories he had uncovered in his fourth step work. In particular, he remembered times when his father verbally abused him for wanting to do normal teenage activities because these activities took him out of the home and away from helping his mother with his disabled sister.

He remembered feeling angry, guilty, frustrated, and sad. He remembered the "lessons" he learned. This was the beginning of his character defect, rooted in the hurt he experienced when love was withheld. These debilitating lessons included core be-liefs like, "Keep your mouth shut"; "If you want something badly, you won't get it"; "Hide your angry feelings"; "Don't ex-press them or you will be punished"; "Try to forget about what you really want to avoid frustration."

Most deeply rooted of all was the belief that somehow he was unworthy of love. Somehow he was fundamentally bad and it would be his fate to go through life never really accepted and cared for. As a result, he felt a deep sense of guilt just for want-ing to be loved.

This was the toxic shame that impeded Sean's emotional de-velopment. He had already come to the understanding that his character defects of non-assertiveness, resentment, stuffing his anger, anxiety, sense of inadequacy, and low self-esteem were all rooted in this core belief. Now, at Step Six, he had to become ready to have God remove this powerful obstacle to his own health and happiness.

The reason these beliefs are called core beliefs is they color all kinds of experiences. They shape the way you experience events and how you store them in your memory. When similar situations come along later in life, you quickly associate the new event with the same interpretation. This sets up a repetitive cy-cle that can last a very long time.

AWARENESS

Sean's recovery required him to examine those memories he had uncovered in his Step Four Inventory. Each painful recollec-tion involving the core belief that he was unworthy of love and respect contributed to the building up of this belief.

For example, Sean asked his father if he could go out for the football team. He was told he was selfish for even wanting to. How could he think of himself when his mother had no help taking care of Terry? This, according to his father, proved that he was self-centered, good for nothing, and an unworthy mem-ber of the family.

Naturally, Sean was deeply hurt. Not just because he was unable to do what he wanted, but because he experienced the withholding of love from his father. Love, he learned, was given conditionally depending on whether he pleased his father or not. Of course he wanted his father's love. So he adopted behaviors which he hoped would be pleasing, withholding his true feelings, stuffing his anger, and so on.

As an outsider you might be thinking to yourself, "That's crazy!" And you'd be right in a certain way. A lot of core beliefs are not very rational, they don't make sense to someone living outside the family setting. But remember, as children, we are formed in the image and likeness of our parents. We depend on the older members of the family to teach us who we are and how we are to live. The family teaches the child his or her identity.

IMAGING AND HEALING OF MEMORIES

The spiritual readiness which Sean sought in Step Six required him to accept his Higher Power's unconditional love for him in place of the conditional love offered by his parents and others. In working with the memory of the football incident specifically, Sean examined each dysfunctional core belief and allowed the light of God's love and truth to shine into his memory. In doing this he started the process of healing and reclaiming his inner child.[1] Your inner child is the sum of your childhood memories, both happy and painful. Knowing and nurturing your inner child is an important way to heal painful memories and become ready to release your character defects.

It takes a sufficiently strong ego to do the memory work described here. The mind's reason for shutting out memories can serve to protect the person from overwhelming grief and sadness. Because he had worked the previous five steps, Sean was mentally and emotionally ready to engage the painful memories of his past. He had enough psychological and spiritual support from friends, his sponsor, and God to tackle this next step. If you find dealing with your own memories is still too painful, consider whether your trust in your Higher Power is strong enough now and whether you currently experience enough support from trusted friends to successfully face these painful memories.

To begin the process of healing his inner child Sean had to relive his memories exactly as they happened. He had to revisit the scene of the crime. But this time instead of being utterly helpless in the face of his father's words and his own interpretation as a child, Sean prayed for a healing of the memory, for right understanding and love in place of distorted thoughts and anger. In this way he began to parent and nurture his inner child.

As he replayed the event in his mind, he heard a voice say, "Keep your mouth shut, stuff your anger."

Confident of God's power to restore him to health, he was able to answer back, "My anger is a valid feeling. I may not choose to express it right now if I would be hit or verbally abused further. But I know it's okay to be angry. I have a right to experience it and to express it."

He repeated the process until the tape changed, until he altered the way he remembered the incident with a more balanced interpretation. Then he moved on to the next dysfunctional core belief.

He heard, "Try to forget about what you really want so that you won't be disappointed and frustrated."

In response he said, "It is not wrong to want something. It is not wrong to express my wants and needs."

He heard, "I am not worthy to be loved by my father. Somehow, I am not worthy to be loved at all."

In response he said, "I know that I am worthy to be loved and that I am loved by God unconditionally, no matter what has happened or will happen."

Sean experienced the unconditional love of his Higher Power for him as a child in each of these hurtful memories. He felt his anger toward his father melt as he experienced the power of God's love providing for his unfulfilled need in each hurtful memory. The long-held anger was released because the memory no longer had the power to rob Sean of self-esteem. That flowed from his relationship with God. As the energy of the anger in the memory receded, so did the resentments.

The most difficult part of the healing process for Sean was reliving the hurtful memories of Jennifer. They were the freshest, most painful memories. He had less confidence in himself and God. His fears and doubts caused him to hold on to his resentments. They still seemed to serve some purpose.

As he remembered conflicts with his wife, Sean's anger intensified. The most painful part of the memory was the way in which the conflict ended. Unresolved, torn, and fractured arguments which led nowhere were the rule rather than the exception. Each time Jennifer cut off the discussion by leaving or throwing up her hands and saying, "Enough!" Sean recognized a familiar feeling and image running through his mind. He felt the same feeling of abandonment he experienced when his father drank. He had the image of a large brick wall crashing down between Jennifer and himself.

The wall between him and his father left him with feelings of helplessness, hopelessness, abandonment, and deep hurt. Sean made the connection between the intensity of the anger he felt toward his father—and the deeply rooted hurt behind it—with the intensity of the anger he felt toward Jennifer when he felt emotionally abandoned by her.

It was back to the drawing board. The most poignant memories Sean had turned up in his childhood were rooted in the very same feeling of abandonment which he re-experienced every time he and Jennifer had a blowout. Their arguments always ended with Jennifer cutting off the exchange in response to Sean's intense anger.

As Sean's insight increased he also began to feel guilt, rooted in both toxic and healthy shame. The toxic shame was generated by self put-downs which rang through his mind. "I'm a fool for letting myself get so out of control that I yell at Jennifer even after she's crying. How can I be so insensitive?"

Sean's task was to answer these put-downs with honest self-appraisal that produces healthy shame, or the acceptance of responsibility for his part in the conflict.

"I'm not a fool. I'm not worthless. I am worthy to be loved, even though I have made mistakes. I want to become aware of when 'the wall' comes into my mind and then have the strength and insight to feel those feelings without blaming Jennifer for them. They are my feelings from my experience. I want Jennifer to help me work through them, but I can't force her to."

The process of imaging was helpful to Sean in addressing each of the hurtful memories he uncovered in his Step Four work. In the process he forgave the spiritual debt Jennifer owed him. This, in turn, opened the door for God's love to heal the toxic shame that robbed him of his self-esteem. In this way he became spiritually ready—that is willing—to have God remove his defects of character.

STEP SIX: STEP GUIDE

In Step Six you begin intervention with the roots of your character defects, especially the ones most hurtful to your spouse. This is not done to appease your spouse or make everything "okay." Rather, it is a part of your program done for yourself, by yourself and your Higher Power. It is impossible to do a good Step Six without having done Steps One through Five.

In the first three steps you let go of the obsession with your spouse's character defects and released responsibility for them. You placed your own life and needs in God's care. You chose to depend on God for the fulfillment of your needs rather than your spouse. In this way, God took rightful first place in your life. Your former obsessions with your spouse were broken.

With Steps Four and Five you acknowledged the presence of your own character defects. These acquired defects arose from the hurtful experiences in your childhood and adolescence. They resulted from instincts misdirected; that is, they come from the dysfunctional and ineffective drive to fulfill your needs by yourself, for yourself, without the acknowledgment of God as the ultimate source of need fulfillment.

Now, with Step Six you become entirely ready to have God remove your defects of character. Using the self-awareness gained through Steps Four and Five, the first part of Step Six requires a detailed look at your acquired character defects. These defects range from mild (for example, telling half-truths for your advantage) to severe (for example, indifference and insensitivity to your spouse and others' pain).

This detailed look at your character defects must also include an honest evaluation of which defects are most hurtful to your spouse. For Sean, the defect was his tendency to vent anger at Jennifer even after she was hurt and crying. Upon closer examination Sean discovered venting anger in such a destructive way resulted from the way he handled his anger at Jennifer in general. He allowed his anger to build to the point of explosion. The core defect he had to work on was his lack of assertiveness.

PART ONE

Write the following Step Six work in your journal:

1. Using your Step Four Inventory, list your acquired character defects.

2. Identify the character defects most damaging to your marriage.

PART TWO

The next part of Step Six is becoming spiritually and emotionally ready to have God remove the character defects most damaging to your marriage. Spiritual readiness has to do with the willingness to give up your most cherished defects of character. It requires complete forgiveness of the emotional and spiritual debt your spouse owes you. Use your Step One work to remind you of each time your spouse has hurt you.

Write the following Step Six work in your journal:

1. List all the offenses, real and imagined, your spouse has knowingly or unknowingly committed against you.

2. Completely erase the legitimate spiritual and emotional debt your spouse owes you by praying the following prayer:

God, You have completely and absolutely forgiven me for my offenses against You, against my spouse, and against myself. I have accepted and completely forgiven myself for these offenses also. I now ask for the strength of character to completely forgive my partner for every offense I have ever held against him/her in my heart. I forgive completely by Your power, not mine. I forgive as completely as You forgive me. Amen.

PART THREE

To complete the task of becoming spiritually and emotionally ready to release your character defects, it is important to carefully review your Step Four work and enter into the process of healing hurtful memories. Begin with your childhood memories. Work through adolescence. End with the hurtful memories you have listed and forgiven your spouse for.

Use your Inventory Sheets from the Step Four (p. 66) section of your journal. You will now complete the work begun in Step Four by asking your Higher Power to help you relive these hurtful memories and to heal each one. Remember, these memories form the foundation and roots of your character defects. You are asking God to heal the toxic shame left over from these memories. You do so by rationally reforming the dysfunctional core beliefs that remain. Use the following format in your journal. Begin with a prayer like this one:

God, as I re-experience these hurtful memories, I ask You for the courage I will need. Please provide the willingness I lack to forgive each of my loved ones who have hurt me. Please provide the guidance I need in finding out how I have been scarred by these incidents, how I still strive to fill the unfulfilled needs I had back then in destructive ways even now. Help me to respond with strength to the

false voices within me that rob me of self-esteem and per-
petuate my character defects. I release my needs, my
character defects to Your care. I know that You want to
heal them. Amen.

Sean's Step Six healing of hurtful memories work regarding
his father is filled in as an example.

Situation	How I Felt Rate 1–100	Lesson Learned (Core Belief)	Acquired Character Defect	Rational Response	New Feeling & Perception Rate 1–100
PERSON: My dad I wanted to go out for the football team, but when I told my father, he screamed at me, saying I was selfish for leaving my mom alone to take care of my sister in the afternoon. He said I was self-centered, good-for-nothing, and that all I ever thought of was what I wanted.	Angry – 90	1. "Keep your mouth shut."	Non-assertiveness	"My anger is a valid feeling. I may choose not to express it to avoid punishment but I know it is okay and it is okay to feel it and express it."	Angry – 40 "My dad had no right to speak to me that way."
	Guilty – 80	2. "Stuff your anger to avoid punishment."	Stuffing anger		Compassion – 50 "My father spoke out of his anger and pain."
	Frustrated – 100	3. "If you want something badly you won't get it."	Resentment	"It is not wrong to want something. It is not wrong to express my needs and wants."	Sad – 50 Compassion for myself – 50 "I lost so much that other kids got. But I made it through anyway."
	Sad – 75	4. "Try to forget about what you want."	Sense of inadequacy		
		5. "My dad has withdrawn his love because I'm unworthy of his love."	Low self-esteem	"I know that I am worthy to be loved and I am loved by God unconditionally no matter what has happened or will happen."	Loved – 80 A Sense of Peace – 80 "It wasn't my fault. When my dad emotionally abandoned me it was because of what was going on with him, not because of me."
			Toxic shame		

Situation	How I Felt Rate 1–100	Lesson Learned (Core Belief)	Acquired Character Defect	Rational Response	New Feeling & Perception Rate 1–100
PERSON: Jennifer We were in New York for the holidays. Jennifer and I walked all over town. I went along with it because I knew it would make her happy. And she knew it wasn't my thing. It was for her. I finally couldn't take anymore and I left for the hotel. She came in screaming at me. I screamed back at her.	Angry – 90 Guilty – 80 Frustrated – 80 Sad – 80	1. "I can't give her an inch or she'll take a mile! She's spoiled rotten. She throws tantrums when she doesn't get her way." 2. "I should have been able to avoid this, but I can't." 3. "We're right back where we started. Slip up once with her and everything is forgotten." 4. "Maybe she's right. I'm an adult child of an alcoholic and I don't know how to fully give of myself."	Non-assertiveness Stuffing anger Sense of inadequacy Resentment Willingness to assume the worst Low self-esteem Toxic shame	"I can give an inch or as much as I think is best. She can demand, but I can decide how and when I feel good about giving to her. I can be assertive." "I want to become aware of the critical points when my anger and frustration are getting high so I can avoid these situations. I know sometimes I'll fail. But I won't condemn myself for it." "We are not 'right back where we started.' I have learned from these experiences. I know she has too, even if she doesn't admit it." "I am able to give and receive love. I know it and I think she does too. Even if she doesn't recognize it, I know it is true."	Angry – 50 "I don't like the way she demands that I do this or that. But it's not awful or intolerable." Frustration – 50 Guilty – 50 "I do not have a responsibility to try to head off problems. But it's not all my fault. I accept my responsibility. I leave hers to her." Sad – 40 "I want things to be better. I want her to recognize my efforts and the progress we've made. But I know I can't force it." Self-confidence – 80 I can give of myself. I can think through the issues in our relationship and I will continue to take my part of the responsibility as best I can." Loved – 80 A Sense of Peace – 80 "It isn't my fault. When my dad or Jennifer emotionally abandon me it is because of what is going on with them, not because of me."

7

HUMILITY

STEP SEVEN: WE HUMBLY ASKED GOD TO RE-
MOVE OUR SHORTCOMINGS.

Humility is the willingness to accept yourself as you are, nothing more and nothing less. Humility is the rational response to
the powerlessness you experience in your life because you seek
to do the good you can do, while acknowledging and accepting
your limitations. Humility derives from your spiritual life. It is a
love for the truth and a willingness to do good, not from fear, but
because you love goodness. Humility lets you see how best to
care for yourself, your spouse, and others.

Humility is one of those things that the moment you think
you've got it you've lost it. It is an ideal you constantly reach for.
Each time you reach a certain level of awareness and transformation, each time you think you have just about got it all together, some new challenge comes along demanding still more
from you. On the one hand, you think, "How can I do any
more?" Yet, when you place your faith in God you find, to your
surprise, you do grow; you can change.

Humility counters the effects of the false self. The false self is
a product of distorted thoughts and beliefs about yourself. The
term "false self" can be misleading, implying you have done
something wrong. It is false because of its limited and distorted
understanding of who you are. The recovery work done up to
this point was aimed at acquiring self-knowledge in order to replace the distorted thoughts and beliefs about yourself with a

healthy, integrated self-image. A healthy self-concept is essential in a healthy marriage. The inventory of Step Four made you aware of your strengths and weaknesses in a balanced way. Step Five brought acceptance of those traits. Step Six took your shortcomings and put them in proper context, whittling them down to their true size and shape. Now you are ready to deal with each shortcoming. Step Seven is the method for changing these shortcomings.

THE TRUE SELF

There are bound to be days in your married life when every decision you make seems to be the wrong one and you find yourself saying, "I'm just not myself today." At any given time you have a certain idea about who you are. You may like that person or you may not. You may want to change parts of your character or you may not. In any case, your self-image is just that, an image or concept. Because it is an abstraction it is a reduction. You are always more as a living person than the idea you have about yourself. This is not to say your self-image is completely erroneous, only incomplete. Behind the mask of the false self projected to the world is your true self.

What is this true self? If the false self is an acquired set of distorted beliefs about yourself, then the true self is the unacquired, or given, truth about yourself. The struggle of day-to-day living may color the way you think about yourself. Your circumstances may influence this self-concept, but they do not recreate you. You do not become a whole new person in every new setting you walk into. Something in you remains stable and constant. This is the uniqueness of your own individuality that you bring to every event and relationship.

The true self is already as it should be. It is not something that is whipped into shape by you. The seed is good already. If you let the seed grow, without distortion or disease, it will become what it is meant to be. Through prayer and meditation the true self is discovered by you and appropriated into your conscious self. Your self-image is adapted as you integrate more and more of your true self. You can carry yourself in different ways, but your true self is what it is. It calls not to be changed but accepted.

The false self is the result of misdirected instincts. The true self is where instincts hit their mark. By practicing a spiritual way of life and trying to overcome the shortcomings of the false self, the true self moves and inspires you to actions and attitudes by which your needs are met. The false self takes your life's energies, distorts them, over-indulges them, and otherwise misuses them. This is what gives you that restless feeling, a general dissatisfaction with your life, like an itching to shed old skin.

By humbly seeking God's intervention in these matters of the false self you do two things. First, humility directs your energies toward what is right and good and not toward what is merely convenient or facile. In this sense, humility initially makes more of a demand on you. Secondly, by seeking God's will you change the center of your thinking from yourself to God. This yields tremendous insight into yourself and the events of your life. The experience of powerlessness and surrender, so feared and distorted by your controlling mind, is experienced as newfound freedom and serenity.

Recall Laura and Bob. She was dumbstruck when Bob suggested she had a mistaken set of priorities. In addition to her family responsibilities as a wife and mother, she also had a part-time job and was going to school. When she volunteered to chair a committee for a local charity, Bob put his foot down.

"You aren't home enough as it is! We rarely get a chance to be together without having to rush off somewhere. The house doesn't look like it should. You come home at night in a frazzle and still you want to do more. When is it going to stop?"

"How dare you try to tell me what I should or should not do!" Laura retorted. "You are always trying to control me."

Sifting through the issues and emotions, Laura caught herself saying, "I'll show him." This rang a bell. She stopped and asked herself, "Am I trying to prove something to him?"

Laura decided she was indeed competing with Bob. She admitted that she was insecure. She did not want others to think of her as "just a housewife." For her that was a put-down. Yet deep within her she saw that it was she who was degrading herself. She perceived herself to be nothing special and so there was an insatiable hunger for prestige and accomplishment.

INNER WISDOM

Renewal and healing of your marriage relationship corresponds to the affirmation and appropriation of your true self into all of the aspects of your life. Prayer and meditation, essentials for this spiritual awakening, are the dialogue between your true self and God. He knows you as you truly are. And so, as you glean from God what is right for you, there is an accompanying wisdom guiding your choices. As you see what is right for you there is an imperative which says, "Live according to that true self. This is what will lead you to happiness and fulfillment." Humility is the essential virtue for this inner wisdom to develop since it bespeaks a basic willingness to learn and grow. Healing, recovery, and growth imply change. As John Henry Newman said, "To live is to change and to be perfect is to have changed often."

This inner wisdom speaks to you. Learn to rely on it. Give yourself to it and find yourself moving safely into new territory. Asking God to remove your shortcomings incorporates a prayer to replace those shortcomings with character strengths that will engender intimacy in your marriage.

Ironically, it is conflict, such as you experience in your marriage, that encourages this inner dialogue. It puts you in touch with your true self. In the pinch of conflict your pride is hurt, your will is contradicted and challenged. This causes you to reflect on your own position, your actions and attitudes. When met by an opposing force, how will you respond?

Reflection means you observe yourself as though you were an outsider, being conscious of yourself in an objective way.

What, if anything, should you change about your attitudes and the actions you take, and so on? Next comes a moment of decision. You recognize you are not just an outsider but a participating subject, and therefore, you must make a decision and act. While just thinking about something, however, you can harbor a variety of conflicting thoughts. It is only when you actually decide to act that you have to make a choice. Conflict, then, commits you to a particular course of action. It forces you to decide what is your deepest concern.

Communication often breaks down at this point. You do not want to commit yourself too soon, so you become vague and noncommittal. To resolve conflict a further risk and investment must be taken. You have to risk divulging more of your true thoughts and feelings. Married partners often complain their spouses do not understand them. Yet this is sometimes because issues are not as obvious to one partner as they appear to the other.

Conflict places a demand on you to say what you mean, to be explicit about what you assume and believe. This makes you vulnerable. Simply putting a thought into words and sharing it requires a choice about which words to use to accurately describe what is going on inside of you. Even if you do not say it exactly right the first time, trying to articulate the problem clarifies the issues for both listener and speaker. This is why in Step Seven you explicitly ask God for help. The disease has to be accurately diagnosed before the doctor can prescribe the correct medicine.

The Moral Inventory of Step Four was a kind of formalized reflection with yourself. Its aim was to bring the problem into focus. No doubt you have gained some inner wisdom as a result. You saw some of your choices were not in accord with your deepest desires. They missed the mark. Something less than your true self colored your actions. Perhaps you preferred to look good in your spouse's eyes. Perhaps you wanted to cover over some other mistakes. The humble recognition of these errors does not produce shame as much as insight, and therefore, is a blessing or strengthening for you. For the humble person, this is an opportunity to correct whatever is blocking the fulfillment of God's will which leads to happiness. The specific situations where these events take place, the kinds of persons they take place with, point out the falseness of the false self. They also give clues to the true self that presses to be heard.

Every conscious action can be an expression of either your true inner self or of some adopted role. This is not to say some roles are not functional or useful. Indeed, that is why you adopted them. They fulfill some purpose. However, it is important to make the role serve the whole person (the true self), not the other way around. The task is to alter the adopted role that does not fully suit the needs of your true self rather than bottle up the true self in a role that is inadequate.

This can be the case with couples who have been married for some time. They get used to each other. They adopt routine patterns of behavior toward one another and for a time they feel comfortable with their roles. However, each partner's true self keeps pressing for greater and greater expression. The true self wants to step out of the boundaries prescribed by the false self. Changing roles inevitably causes friction. In families, it means everyone in the family must adapt their role as well. Even families of just two people are complete units. Nothing can happen that does not have an effect on everyone else.

Humility, the willingness to accept yourself as you are—nothing more and nothing less—makes awareness and transformation happen. First of all, to make progress in removing shortcomings, *willingness* not *willfulness* is needed. The willful mind thinks, now that you have this list of faults, you can simply go down the list one by one and fix each defect. The willful mind also thinks it is not a Higher Power that will heal your marriage, but your willpower and ego strength. Here again, the controlling mind tries to regain the power given up by acceptance and surrender. Except now instead of thinking, "If only he or she would change," you are saying to yourself, "If only *I* would change." Willingness is the openness to change. It does not say by whose power change will take place. It is very easy to slip back into thinking, "It all depends on me." It doesn't!

Secondly, in trying to improve yourself, you can become preoccupied with yourself, tending to every detail as though remodeling a house. In humbly asking God to remove your shortcomings, self-consciousness recedes into the background. It does not disappear, but defers to that spontaneous and indefinable true self. At any given moment you may want more of something or less of something. You may feel painful yearning as your own desire for change is frustrated. Humility will bring you serenity, accepting what is at that moment beyond your power to change. It is in God's power and God's time that your shortcomings will be removed.

The willingness to understand is an attitude that will lead to understanding. The two link together. Acceptance of yourself, as you are right now, with strengths and weaknesses, humbly puts you in touch with what you are reasonably able to do at any given moment. In this you must rest.

THREE-DIMENSIONAL LIVING

In conflict it is easy to think with an "either/or" mentality: "Either I am right and she is wrong or I must be wrong and she is right. I don't want to be wrong, so . . ." The humility implied by Step Seven circumvents this trap by making marriage a three-way partnership.

You are a three-dimensional person. First, you have that part of you which you are conscious of. Your *conscious self* is limited by the extent of your own awareness, so in this sense it is your false self. It is constantly being reformulated. It is a limited concept. A healthy self-image includes the humble recognition of certain limited powers you do have. These are the gifts and talents you have naturally or have learned, including social skills, creative skills, powers of affection and reasoning, judgment, physical strength, and so on. The sense you have of your own uniqueness and value is what enables you to contribute to your marriage relationship. A strong, realistic appreciation for yourself as a unique individual is essential for a healthy marriage.

Low self-esteem and a poor self-concept lead to excessive dependence on your partner. Your husband or wife can feel smothered in your neediness, drained by the constant need to prop up your self-esteem. The quality of self-esteem enables you to assert yourself, to carry yourself in a way that others will see exactly who you are and what you want and need. In working to remove shortcomings, you are not aiming to deny any real part of you—especially if it is a strength! Claim whatever your strength is; to do otherwise would be false humility.

The second dimension, as has been explained, is the *true self*. This includes things you are conscious of and things you are unconscious of but are part of you anyway, what is unique to you as an individual and what is commonly shared with others. Just because you are an individual does not mean you are somehow a species all unto yourself. Your true self also includes a common nature that links you to the rest of humanity, connecting you to every other human person. It recalls your link to the universe, to the environment, to God, to your spouse, to your family, and so on. You can only act in accord with this common nature, no matter how much you may wish otherwise.

Unacceptance of this connection can lead to over-identification with a particular role you play. Perfectionism and rigidity develop as a person sees his or her whole life defined in terms of a certain role. For example, the woman who sees herself only as a mother and relates to her spouse only as the father of her children, who refers to him always as "Daddy," fails to recognize she is like every other woman with adult needs. Her true self yearns for companionship among her peers, for intimacy with friends, and for intimacy with her husband as her mate.

The third dimension is the *humble self*. This is the person struggling to know the true self, wrestling with character defects, and so on. This is the person who stands needy, wanting to be made whole, wanting to enter into marriage freely, decisively, spontaneously. This is the person who lives each day with partial vision, yet who continues to act on faith. The humble self makes no bones about its failures or successes. Both the good times and the bad can be instructive, and that is all that matters.

You may ask yourself what the difference is between the true self and the humble self. In fact, they are the same. Yet, the term *humble self* illustrates the spiritual journey of discovery that takes place over time. The humble self is aware of its dependence on God for progress and upon others for fulfillment as a human being. "No man is an island," said John Donne.

The humble self is the person aware that he or she must walk by faith, trusting his or her own judgment, having confidence in himself or herself, yet not taking that confidence too far. Humility is a bit like standing in a spotlight. You are free to move in any direction and still be in the light—up to a point. After that point you start to move out of the light. Humility recognizes the limitations of your own strengths, knowledge, and virtues. Humility does not absolutize your own points of view, yet neither is it willing to move too far to the other extreme and deny any good in you. The shortcomings you have do not necessarily doom you to a life of misery. Power to overcome them lies not in you but in God who can endure all things. The humble self can sustain the humiliation of your self-image while continuing to search for fuller expression of the true self. The true self lives peacefully in the knowledge that God is truth and love and brings only good to those who wait.

THREE-DIMENSIONAL LOVE

Love also has three dimensions. Each one has its own purpose and value.

The first dimension is *passion* or erotic love. This is not just sweat and hormones. It is the wonderful strength that comes to you when you are with that special person who wholly accepts and embraces you. When you give yourself to another person in passionate love you feel empowered. Self-confidence is built up. You sense your life is truly valuable and affirmed. Energy is drawn from your lover. Expressions such as "hunger" and "aching" are commonly used to describe the sense of exchange, of taking into yourself the life of the other person. Passion carries you away. You forget about the rest of the world. You are focused exclusively on the experience of intimacy with your lover. Images of flight, of being released from ordinary everyday constraints are common. You feel as though you could conquer the world.

A different but equally powerful experience of love is the experience of *compassion* or agape love. This too is a unitive experience, not just with one person but with all peoples, indeed with all of creation. You become spiritually aware of what holds you in common rather than what differentiates you from one another. You are profoundly alert to the environment that sustains you, captivated by the wonder of everything outside of yourself. Your self-awareness recedes into self-forgetfulness. You are overwhelmed with the sense of belonging, of being with your own kind, of coming home. It is a casting off of your concerns for yourself brought on by the discovery of something more beautiful and vital beyond yourself.

Unchecked passion leads to a domineering mentality. Imposing or controlling partners may suffer from the addictive powers of passion. Everyone loves to feel powerful and strong. But what keeps power and strength in balance is compassion, the sense of being in harmony with others. By the same token, compassion can be distorted without a balance of passion. Self-assertiveness does not contradict humility. It is a passionate act on behalf of what you value and care for. Without passion a person may become mired by indecision.

A sound marriage requires the ability to respond passionately as well as compassionately. There must be enough ego strength to be an active, working partner in the marriage, while also appreciating the needs of your spouse. Both are expressions of love in its different forms. Your marriage, like the humble self, is a mixture of successes and failures in responding to your own needs and the needs of your partner.

Love, as humility in marriage, is friendship in its most profound sense. Friendship is the love between two equals. Partners in a marriage are equally in need of both autonomy and intimacy. A friend strives to be a companion, to provide what will aid the other. In marriage, this sometimes takes the form of passion, sometimes the form of compassion. Friends disagree, yet are humble enough to accept the differences out of respect for their individual characters. Marriage partners must also be humble enough to recognize every difference of opinion is not an act of infidelity. Friends stand shoulder to shoulder through their common journey of life. Husband and wife are partners in a mutual enterprise of happiness and fulfillment.

Yet, conflict can escalate to where neither partner is hearing the other. Both are passionately set on defending their own point of view. Wisdom has to set in and show one or the other that compromise will not diminish them. That is why you have to be in touch with your true self, to know your partner's differing points of view do not threaten you. An expression of understanding or compassion can lovingly dislodge the impasse. Humility seeks the wisdom to know when it is time to assert oneself and when it is time to back off. Both are aspects of love for yourself (self-esteem) and love for your spouse.

HUMILITY IN MARRIAGE

The supreme goal of marriage is set forth in the oft-repeated phrase, "and the two shall become one." The appeal of married love is that someone unconditionally accepts you, prizes you, welcomes you. Ideally, within the walls of matrimony you experience that belonging, that freedom from the competition, criticism, and put-down of the world.

The yearning for this profound unity is deeply rooted. From the moment you are separated from the womb this quest for reunion begins. The child is most at home at Mother's breast or always careful never to stray far from Daddy's side. Within this interaction of dependence and independence the personality of the child emerges. A creative tension develops like the child's initial steps. First tentative expressions of independence contrast the usual clinging to the safety of the parent. As the child matures, the ability to alternate from one to the other becomes stronger.

The love of husband and wife moves between two poles, unity and individuality. Unity is juxtaposed to the independence and self-determination of the two individuals. Like changing tides, couples must adapt to the prevailing mood. In conflict with each other, the couple is painfully reminded that they are not one mind, one heart, one body. That remains an ideal they strive for. They are two distinct persons, with varying opinions and wishes. Each must make a choice to remain in the partnership, which demands a sacrifice of absolute independence. On the other hand, the healthy development of the marriage is complemented by the individual activities of the partners. Marriages are strengthened when partners bring to the relationship experiences acquired outside of their roles as spouses.

The three dimensions of the self (conscious self, true self, and humble self) correspond to the three dimensions of being in relationship: Passion, Compassion, and Friendship. The strength of your ego—that positive, powerful self-regard—drives you into a relationship. It calls you to commit yourself, to act on the love you feel. Within the relationship, passion moves you to exercise your gifts and talents and to express yourself fully and sincerely.

Passionate expression of your individuality calls for a complementary expression of compassion or understanding from your spouse. Compassion empathizes with the needs of another person. Empathy understands what another person is searching for and permits freedom of expression. When your partner is feeling the need to assert, to distinguish, or to express himself or herself, compassion allows you to share the attention, to recede into the background for a time. If you are truly in touch with your true self through prayer and meditation, there is no fear that your own individuality will be overpowered by the strength of your partner. It cannot be taken from you. It is you.

ASKING GOD TO REMOVE YOUR SHORTCOMINGS

God loves perfectly. That is, God is perfectly passionate and compassionate. By humbly asking God to remove your short-comings, you are in essence asking Him to make your choices perfectly loving. Humility recognizes that at times the loving thing to do is to speak up, at other times to button up. Wisdom will help you decide. The proper mode of love (passion or compassion) will power you through the troubled waters of conflict while serving both the needs of your true self and the needs of your spouse.

God's own love is humble. During the day the light of the sun outshines the light of the stars. So, too, God's love would over-power any individual person's love were God not so deferential. This is why at times God's love seems distant and dark. It is why we pray and pray and troubles do not seem to go away. Some-thing else is missing. If God's power is to increase in your life, your power must decrease. The humble prayer that seeks the truth will be met with a quick reply. Remember, the prayer "Not my will, but Thy will be done" is a promise of humility, to seek what is truly right and good as opposed to what seems to you to be correct.

THE SALESMAN

Paul and Sue are a couple who have been married for more than twenty years. Sue complained that Paul was cold and dis-tant toward her. Paul denied it. "She is just overly sensitive. No one has ever made that complaint to me before. In fact, just the opposite."

Still, her comment disturbed him. Paul met regularly with a support group of friends to discuss what was going on in one another's lives. He told them what Sue had said. Their response was surprising.

They did not agree nor disagree with Sue. They suggested that Paul take some time to look at himself honestly and thoroughly. They suggested that he pray for the openness to discover something about himself that he was not willing to learn but that would help him and his marriage in the long run.

After days of reflection the light started to come to him. He was at work one day when an old high school buddy happened to walk in as a client. The two of them were happily surprised. They spent a lot of time catching up on old times and kidding each other. Paul noticed how awkward it felt getting down to business with someone who had been his "partner in crime" during the old school days.

"The salesman-to-client relationship is well defined," he thought later. "You want something from the client and the client wants something from you. It's utilitarian. When my old buddy walked in it felt unnatural for me to slip on the 'mask of salesman,' or at least it took a conscious effort when it came to someone I knew as a friend.

"That experience made me realize that what I enjoy about being a salesman is the hunt. You try to put your best foot forward. You try to show them the best sides without being 'hard sell' about it. You try to make the customer feel like they are in charge, while steering them down the direction you want. It isn't that you lie or misrepresent yourself, but you know not to say too much. A good salesman develops an instinct about what the other person is thinking and tries to always be a step ahead of them. Then once the deal is cut the relationship comes to a conclusion. Everybody's happy.

"Marriage, though, requires a whole different set of instincts. And a lot of what comes across to Sue as cold and distant is my failure to shift gears. I relate to her, sometimes, as though she were a customer. The instinct to create an impression or to leave a specific perception on the customer is a habit I employ unconsciously with her sometimes. In marriage, you can't calculate every word or gesture. You have to be yourself. Sometimes I am not pleasant, competent, or appealing.

"When I am tired or pressed for time I notice my strongest habits take over. I become 'the salesman.' It isn't always intentional or conscious, but I do admit it is a form of controlling and manipulation."

The rules of the marketplace became such a part of Paul's style of interacting with people he did not realize he was even doing it. Any time Sue would sit down to share a personal thought or express a personal feeling, it seemed she was being either dismissed as unimportant or her point of view was knocked down by a series of retorts. Unlike a business relationship, your spouse is not after you for something. Often, he or she is simply after you: your time, your affection, your love. Paul recognized that in other circumstances his wit and charm attracted people to him, but at home it was taken as a "brush off" or arrogance.

"It was a humbling experience. I first thought, 'How can I change my personality? That's just the way I am.' I didn't distinguish between my true self and the role I was playing. I had to admit that the traits I learned through business I had adopted for the purpose of succeeding in business, as a means of success. These traits were not in fact my true personality. They were tools of my trade.

"I began to ask God to make me consciously aware of these traits, to know when and under what circumstances I relied on them. I saw that I had a variety of choices in the way I responded to people. I let only a certain part of me show in my relationships with others."

Sue described the problem this way: "I sometimes felt that Paul was holding back from me, as if there was something he should tell me, but he didn't want me to know. When I would take the risk and share something personal then he would react to my feelings or comments. I rarely sensed he was contributing equally, as freely or as deeply. I thought for a while that was just a man's way. But later I felt like I was being taken advantage of, like he was selling me a 'bill of goods.' "

Luckily, Paul was able to exercise a degree of humility with regard to himself. He was willing to struggle with Sue's complaint until he saw it from her point of view. He did not simply reject it. Because he was able to be honest with himself about his own shortcomings he could seek the counsel of others openly. Rather than being embarrassed or self-conscious, Paul invited Sue to explore the problem together.

In accepting the challenge, Paul grew in self-knowledge, which helped him not only to be a better husband but a better salesman. So many clues about your true self are provided for you by the way people respond to you and through the things they say. In your quickness to defend your self-image you may miss an important insight. Humility is a willingness to see and accept the truth in whatever form it takes. Transformation occurs by acting in response to the truth you discover.

STEP GUIDE: STEP SEVEN

Asking God to remove your shortcomings is also an invitation to grow in virtues, in personal strength and wisdom. It does not mean you will become anything you do not want to be. Some people think, "If you are being good you're not having any fun." The difficulties you are having in your marriage cannot be much fun. So, maybe it is not a matter of trying harder, but trying smarter.

In this exercise the object is to make a firm act of trust in your Higher Power, in the God that loves you and knows you even better than you know yourself. Take each shortcoming that you are aware of at this moment and ask for God's help in overcoming it, so that you can live from your true self and thereby love with a sincere heart.

GUIDED MEDITATION/PRAYER

Sit near a window or in some out-of-the-way spot where you will not be disturbed. You may want to repeat this meditation several times. Put your body in a comfortable position. Pause for a moment to feel the comfort going through your muscles. Part of your true self includes your body. Be friends with it. Notice any pains or tensions. Relax.

Once your body is relaxed let your mind relax. This may be

more difficult. Thoughts immediately pop up. Things you have forgotten to do invade your thoughts. Let them be like the scenery passing by the car window. They are part of your conscious mind. They pertain to the roles you play. For now, they are not important.

Recall your faith in God. God is love, and God loves you as you are right now. You are as you should be to Him. It is the false self that distorts your thinking and vision of the true self. The power of God's love is there to help you. Are you completely willing to let God love you and heal you?

Express to God aloud your willingness to let Him remove all your shortcomings, anything that prevents you from being the happy, healthy, loving person you are meant to be.

If you have made a Step Four Inventory, take each of the items you uncovered and mention them one by one. For example, you may have uncovered a need for respect. In your honesty and humility you recognize the shortcoming of aggression as you try to satisfy that need. Say, in these or similar words, "Lord, _____ is my weakness; in your time and in your way grant me the virtue of _____.

Once you have gone through the list of shortcomings you are aware of, spend a moment appreciating the life you have been given. Remember, every character defect has a corresponding strength, should you choose to use it in God's way rather than to your own self-serving ends.

The following prayer has been used by many to conclude the taking of this seventh step:

> **"My Creator, I am now willing that You should have all of me, good and bad. I pray that You now remove from me every single defect of character which stands in the way of my usefulness to You and my fellow journeyers. Grant me the strength, as I go out from here, to do Your bidding. Amen."**

8

WILLINGNESS

> **STEP EIGHT: MADE A LIST OF ALL PERSONS WE HAD HARMED AND BECAME WILLING TO MAKE AMENDS TO THEM ALL.**

Now comes a turning point. In fact, it is the main point. All along you have been asking yourself, What can I do to influence my partner for the better? Is there something I can say so that he or she will understand me? Is there something I can do to express my love while also confronting the real troubles in our relationship?

In Step One we asked you to detach yourself from this line of questioning temporarily because of the destructive power of the obsessive mind. You stepped back and acknowledged your obsessive focus on your partner's character defects. Through a personal inventory of yourself, you became aware of the specific ways in which your unfulfilled needs colored your perception of your spouse's attitudes and actions toward you. You humbly acknowledged and took responsibility for the part you play in your marriage, both the good and the bad. The willingness to look at yourself and acknowledge the strengths and weaknesses in your own character gave you a clearer understanding of the strengths and weaknesses of both yourself and your marriage.

Seeing clearly, you must choose wisely. There should be no illusions about who you are and what you are capable of accomplishing in this relationship. Likewise, there should be no impulsive actions, actions taken without forethought and a conscious choice. Now it is time to turn the focus from yourself back toward your marriage. How will you approach your spouse with the goal of healing your marriage?

It takes a lot to make a marriage work. A free choice for the marriage is perhaps the most essential part. It is nonsensical to say that you are forced to love your husband or wife, no matter how long you have been married. The relationship can be a lot of things, but without love it is not a marriage. Love is always a gift that you give. The challenge that faces you at this moment is your own free choice for the marriage. Are you completely committed to the marriage? If so, what are you willing to do to better the relationship?

Commitment to your marriage involves risk. You know you cannot control your spouse. Nevertheless, the awareness of the risks and loss of control, conditioned by past bad experiences, makes committing to the marriage a weighty choice. Why go through it again?

The choice to renew romance in your marriage comes when you have decided the reward is worth the risk. How do you know if it is worth it? Would you be happier with another? Maybe you think you would be. How can you be sure you are not just looking for greener grass that in the long run will be just as hard to chew? Some people simply settle for less. They are afraid; maybe they are lazy. They do not improve their marriage; perhaps they divorce. Either way, they expect less from themselves and others, and consequently, never experience a lasting love.

Clearly, no one can tell you which way you should go. This choice is up to you and God. You have to find the reasons for staying or leaving. The inventory work you have done has given you a clearer picture of yourself and the needs of your marriage. Making the marriage work is a combination of what you know and what you are willing to do. It is a bit like when you first married. You wondered if you were making the right choice. You based your choice on what you knew about the person and what you hoped in. For most newlyweds, it is more hope than knowledge. Now there is more knowledge. You understand your spouse better. In answering the question of whether you are willing to make amends, you have to examine what you hope for.

Restoring your marriage depends on your commitment to the relationship. You will not take the risks necessary for real intimacy in your marriage if you have doubts about its future. Your controlling mind will sabotage half-hearted efforts. Would you be willing to make amends to someone you love? Sure. How do you know whether you love your spouse or not? Tough question. What is love after all?

Perhaps love cannot be defined, but there is always evidence of it. An act of love is always freely given and the giver is in some way fulfilled by it. The reward is in the action itself. For example, there is no practical reason for a kiss. But love is felt by means of a kiss. The one doing the kissing finds pleasure, meaning, and fulfillment in the action.

Another, less romantic example: Let's say you come home and your partner has left you a note, "Honey, please take out the garbage." You hate taking out the garbage! But you think to yourself, "If I do it, at least he or she will think I'm trying to help out." Is this a loving gesture?

Even if you do it muttering all the way, the facts are 1) It did help out; 2) It did send a signal that you are trying to help out. Does this qualify as a loving gesture? A loving gesture does not have to be something you like doing. But if it is a conscious choice to convey an honest intention of love to the other person, yes, it qualifies. The evidence of love is not always given in the feelings you have or the way you think about someone, but in what you do. Your partner may make you mad; you may do something with mixed emotions; but what you actually do gives more evidence of your love than anything else. How do you know whether you love your spouse? By what you are willing to do.

BECOMING WILLING

Willingness to make amends for wrongs you are responsible for is a specific act of love that has a positive effect on your marriage. Making amends, even for something small, sends a good message to your spouse and increases your self-esteem. The more specific you are about the amends you need to make the better. Even more important are your subsequent actions. After making amends for past wrong-doing it is important to back your apology up with sincere actions. The actual amends making and perseverance are the substance of Steps Nine and Ten. Step Eight deals with willingness. What if you are not *willing* to make amends? The work of Step Eight involves understanding and overcoming the unwillingness to make amends to your spouse.

In general, the unwillingness to make amends to your spouse is rooted in the remaining resentments you hold against him or her. As we have seen, the destructive character defects in your personality are the result of the hurtful experiences of the past. Although you handed these experiences over to God for healing in Step Six, your unfulfilled needs remain. This is where your unwillingness to make amends to your spouse comes from.

Part of a healthy marriage contract is an implicit agreement, "I will help you to fulfill your needs. I want you to help me to fulfill my needs." Your partner has not lived up to this bargain!

The character defect in your spouse—the one over which you are powerless—continues to hurt you right in your weakest spot: your unfulfilled need. Because you have exposed your deepest emotions and weakness to your spouse, you are vulnerable. This is necessary in order to have your deepest needs met. However, you find yourself unwilling to make amends for the ways in which you have hurt your spouse because if you were to apologize first you would lose the power to make your spouse fulfill your need. Admission of your responsibility in the relationship and the fact that you have not done such a great job fulfilling your spouse's needs would seem to be an admission that you have been wrong—and your spouse has been right—all along.

The fact is both you and your spouse have unfulfilled needs. Both your needs and your spouse's needs are important. The irrational line of thinking, however, is often as follows:

- "My spouse *should* fulfill all my needs for love and affection."

- "My partner *should* make me feel good about myself."

- "My spouse *should* be able to put up with my character defects just as well as I put up with his or hers."

- "My partner *should* live up to the basic and reasonable expectations I have of a husband or wife."

The problem is not that wanting these things is somehow bad or dysfunctional. The problem is that each dysfunctional belief fails to recognize your spouse's freedom to make a choice to love you as you would like to be loved. It is a free choice. It cannot be forced. The following rational responses recognize this freedom:

- "I *want* my spouse to fulfill my need for love and affection. I know that I can receive love and affection in other relationships too."

- "I feel good about myself on my own. I *want* my partner to affirm my self-esteem."

- "I *want* my spouse to be patient with me and I will be patient with him or her."

- "I have legitimate expectations of my spouse. Even if he or she does not fulfill them now, I still love him or her and I still *want* him or her to make progress on the problem."

Dependency is a part of the dynamic that maintains the old addiction to resentment and the struggle to change your spouse. It demands the fulfillment of needs. *Interdependency* becomes possible in the new and transformed marriage relationship with the abstinence from addictive and destructive behaviors of the past. It asks the fulfillment of needs in your marriage, recognizing the freedom of your spouse to say no. It has been said that the one word an addict hates to hear the most is *no*. This is true, as well, of those who are addicted to the way of thinking that destroys marriages.

When you recognize your spouse's freedom to say no you paradoxically open the way for him or her to say yes. The most rational choice is to give up the power struggle. As long as you demand the fulfillment of your needs and wants, you keep the tug-o-war going.

The work of Step Eight involves overcoming the unwillingness to make amends to your spouse. Unwillingness is a hold on power for some reason, something that must be uncovered and thought out. How strong is that reason? How important is that reason to you in relation to your marriage as a whole? Many of the reasons that underlie irreconcilable differences between spouses are based on irrational thoughts—the situation and the belief you hold about the situation just don't add up. Becoming willing to make amends means unraveling the snafu of irrational thoughts.

IRRATIONAL TRAPS

The following are the most common *irrational traps* couples fall into:

1. Tunnel Vision:[1] You focus on one relatively small detail as a basis for your view of an entire event or situation, for example, "We fought the entire trip."
2. Negative Focus: You attend to the negative and critical communication from your partner. You ignore or misperceive the positive input from your partner. Loving, supportive, encouraging input somehow doesn't count because of all the times your partner was negative or critical.
3. Personalization: You arbitrarily conclude that your partner is trying to hurt you even though there is no real evidence, for example, "She's saying those things specifically to hurt me."
4. Overgeneralization: You take one or a few incidents and conclude that your partner's behavior at those specific times is typical or usual, for example, "He always criticizes me;" "she's never satisfied."
5. Black and White Thinking: You tend to see events in your marriage or qualities of your spouse as totally great or completely horrible. If your partner's performance is not perfect, it

is seen as a complete failure. You become rigid about what you want and the way you want it.

6. Magnification: You tend to exaggerate the severity of a particular situation, for example, "I can't stand it when he yells at me;" "it is terrible that she doesn't show me respect the way I want her to." Your marriage problems are seen as unresolvable and catastrophic.

7. Negative Expectation: You assume that your partner will act out his or her character defect rather than work to improve on it. You expect the worst from your partner. You allow pessimism to color your expectations of your partner as a way to protect yourself from disappointment.

8. Negative Labeling: You move from overgeneralizing about your partner's behavior to a negative label which describes your partner permanently as "a loser," "a jerk," or "a nag." You come to believe your partner can never change.

9. Feelings as Facts: You conclude that if you feel strongly about an issue between you and your partner, it must reflect a fact or a reality in your relationship, for example, "I feel hurt; therefore my partner is deliberately persecuting me," or "I feel angry, so I know my partner is doing something wrong."

10. Mind Reading: You believe you already know what your partner will say, so you don't ask or communicate about certain topics. You assume that you know exactly what your partner is thinking in a given situation. You become angry based on this "knowledge."

11. Should, Must, Have-to Thinking: You use "should," "must," and "have to" statements to coerce your partner to do what you think is best. You use a moralistic tone in communication. You believe you can see what is right and your partner cannot.

12. Negative Orientation: Problem issues begin to dominate your overall perception of your marriage. The mere mention of a difficult or unresolved issue can "ruin" your day or evening together. A negative or critical comment from your partner causes you to discount his or her viewpoint and question his or her sincerity.

The following is a list of *rational responses* you can employ to avoid these traps:

1. Perspective: You place a single negative event in context, as part of an overall picture. "We fought, but not the whole time."
2. Recognize the Positive: You attend to both critical input and positive, loving and supportive communication from your partner. You place more emphasis on the positive since it is what you want more of from your partner.
3. One Hundred Percent Responsibility: You take all of your responsibility and none of your partner's. You avoid inferring your partner's motives and instead focus on your responsibility in the problem area.
4. Reasonable Conclusion: You recognize a specific situation as unique. "He doesn't always criticize. When he does, it usually means he's upset about something . . ."
5. Realistic Thinking: You see your spouse's qualities as they are, with varying degrees of good and bad. You avoid perfectionism. You recognize gray areas. You are more flexible.
6. Moderation in Perception: You do not exaggerate the severity of a problem. You recognize difficulties, yet focus on possible solutions. You recognize and state your wants. "I don't like it when he yells. I want him to stop."
7. Positive Expectation: You make an accurate assessment of each situation. It is more logical to assume an optimistic orientation since positive expectation often leads to positive results.
8. Honest Evaluation: You evaluate qualities considered positive and negative and their provence in both yourself and your partner. "I don't like it when he talks that way about me, but he's not a jerk . . ."
9. Feelings Recognized and Expressed: You realize feelings are important and need to be expressed. You also recognize that feelings do not change or necessarily imply facts.
10. Active Listening: You listen to what your spouse is actually saying and check out your perceptions with him or her.
11. Preference Statements: You prefer certain behavior from your spouse. You do not attempt to coerce behavior by imposing guilt if the behavior is not forthcoming.
12. Realistic Orientation: You focus on the positive aspects of your marriage as well as the negative. Situations and events formerly viewed as exclusively negative are also viewed as challenges and opportunities.

GREG AND JULIE

Greg and Julie are a strong-willed couple. Greg is a successful businessman who prides himself on being intelligent and decisive. He is competent at what he does and has earned the respect of others. Julie is equally intelligent and passionate. She differs from Greg in that she presents her points of view with lots of emotion. You not only know where she stands, you can feel how strongly she holds her position. Greg would rather deal directly with the facts.

Greg becomes upset when Julie is so emotionally involved in what she is saying. It is hard for him to listen to her when she gets that way. "She starts ranting and raving and there's no talking with her. She loses all objectivity. Her feelings become facts. And God help you if you disagree!"

Greg finds this especially annoying when they are with other people. He feels most angry and disrespected when she contradicts him in front of their friends. He describes her at these times as overbearing and brassy.

His usual way of reacting to these situations was to bottle up his anger. He learned long ago that saying what he really thought and felt just made Julie angry. Naturally, his anger would come out in inappropriate ways. He would stuff his anger so long and then blow up at her over a comment he believed to be the "last straw" in a series of comments intended to hurt him. Julie, for her part, complained he did not listen to her. He ignored her and put her down for her opinions. She felt belittled, as though he felt superior to her.

In considering the amends he owed to her, Greg wrestled with what to do. He knew his reaction to her at times was unkind, but he felt she harped on him constantly. He felt he deserved more respect from her than he was getting. Looking at his own character first, he realized there was, indeed, a grain of truth in her complaint. When she became emotional about things, he started tuning her out. He became angry at these times, thinking to himself, "She's saying these things to hurt me! She constantly puts me down and criticizes me."

Greg humbly admitted he had fallen into a number of irrational traps. He would try to correct his irrational thinking as a way of making amends and still get his real need for respect in front of others met. The next time Julie started what he considered "ranting and raving" he would avoid labeling it "ranting and raving." Instead he would interpret the situation something like this: "She is angry about something and I would like to find out what it is."

When he found himself thinking, "She doesn't respect me," he refrained from reasoning from his emotions by saying to himself, "At times she does show me respect. She respects me in many ways. Right now, she is angry. Even when she is angry, however, I would like her to speak to me respectfully."

When he caught himself saying to himself, "She is always criticizing me," he reformed his interpretation by saying, "She doesn't always criticize me. Only when she gets angry about something. I do care about why she is angry." In this way, he avoided overgeneralizing about the situation.

Taking his own measure of responsibility in an argument was difficult for Greg because he was so well practiced at focusing exclusively on Julie's accusations and feeling angry about them. Greg found it important and necessary to forgive Julie for past hurts and to undertake the imaging and healing of memories process described in Chapter Six before tackling his own anger-producing thoughts. After doing the work on the past he became more clearly aware of his thoughts about Julie.

Willingness to make amends for Greg meant dealing with his anger toward Julie. This required that he mentally order the issues in a rational way. First, he thought it unfair that she accused and blamed him instead of listening to his side of the story. Greg prided himself on his ability to get his side of the story across. At the same time, he acknowledged his own reluctance to listen to Julie's side of the issue. Still, he expected Julie to respect him as her husband, especially in front of their friends.

He decided to simply ask Julie to refrain from criticizing him in front of others, rather than demanding it of her. Then, he let go of the issue, realizing that either she would or would not respond. But whether she did or did not was something over which he was powerless. To his surprise, as he let go of his demand for respect, things began to improve. He continued to express his frustration and anger as he felt it, thus avoiding blowups. Julie respected his request and refrained from trying to embarrass him.

Greg was in the process of becoming ready to make amends to Julie. He identified his difficulty in really listening to her as the character defect most hurtful to Julie. He found that his anger was the chief obstacle to his listening. Greg released his resentment toward Julie for past hurts and traced the history of his character defects to the hurtful memories of his adolescence and childhood in his Step Six work. Beginning to make amends to Julie meant changing his thoughts from anger-producing thoughts to more rational thoughts. In the next chapter you will see how he made direct amends by actually changing the way he communicated with Julie.

THE WALL OF RESENTMENT

When the hurtful exchanges between you and your spouse mount up, the memory of your hurt feelings can form a wall which prevents you from really talking about issues and resolving differences. If you are speaking from your pain and hurt feelings nothing can be done to resolve issues. So before you can successfully re-engage with your spouse you must deal with your hurt feelings.

Sean—of Sean and Jennifer in Chapter Four—experienced the sensation of a wall of emotional isolation crashing down between himself and Jennifer whenever she stopped their arguments in the middle by saying, "Enough! I can't take anymore!" Sean knew the isolation and rejection he experienced when Jennifer did this was similar to the hurt he experienced as a child when his father yelled at him. The intensity of Sean's hurt feelings in situations with Jennifer came from past experiences with both his father and with Jennifer. Even though he had allowed God's healing love into these painful memories and had worked to change his perception of each hurtful incident, he still felt emotionally abandoned when Jennifer cut off an argument or ignored his feelings.

Sean realized that one of his defects of character, stuffing anger, tended to fuel the problem. He knew that letting go of this character defect would mean not blaming Jennifer for past hurts and not demanding the fulfillment of his need for emotional nurturance from her. Of course, he still wanted her to stop cutting off arguments and to be open to hearing his hurt feelings when he felt most like expressing them. He knew that asking for this rather than demanding it would be his best chance of receiving it. He also knew that Jennifer would often say no at first because of resentment she held from their many hurtful arguments.

Sean's work to ready himself spiritually to release his defects of character had already borne fruit. As he continued to experience healing of his hurtful memories he became more aware of the sources of his anger with Jennifer. He realized how often his anger was out of proportion to the situation. He recognized that this was largely due to the habit he had learned as a child of "stuffing" his anger, not expressing it but holding it in. Once his anger had built to an unbearable point he would vent it on Jennifer with full force. This is when he found himself becoming emotionally abusive toward Jennifer, when he continued to yell at her even while she sobbed and cried. Such past incidents formed the basis of Jennifer's resentment.

Sean wanted to become completely willing to make amends to Jennifer. The next step was for him to become aware of his anger-producing thoughts and to change them, just as Greg did in his relationship with Julie. In order to accomplish this Sean first had to tune in to his own feelings. He was so well practiced in ignoring his feelings that he concentrated instead on what Jennifer might be thinking. As he became aware of his own thoughts and feelings during conflict, Sean realized that as soon as angry words were exchanged and Jennifer withdrew from him he experienced the image of the wall crashing down between them. It was at that point he felt emotionally abandoned, enraged, and the deep-seated fear that Jennifer would continue to withdraw from him.

Once he was aware of his own thoughts and feelings in the context of an argument, he found he could stop saying angry and hurtful things to Jennifer after she withdrew. He was able to release her. *That is, he admitted his powerlessness over her in an argument.* He was able to talk himself through the situation so that he would not feel as angry and hurt as he had in previous situations. He put the image of the wall into words—words that flashed through his mind in a split second when Jennifer withdrew from an argument.

"She can't do this. She shouldn't do this. She manipulates everything in an argument, and if she can't do that she stops talking and cries. Every argument is a chance for her to complain about me, but she never listens."

Sean realized these thoughts intensified his anger toward Jennifer. But underneath these thoughts were more.

"She doesn't love me. She doesn't care enough about me to stay with an argument. She really has abandoned me. And well she should. I didn't think she would really love me anyway after everything I've done to her. How can I expect to be loved?"

These thoughts caused Sean's hurt feelings to grow. But after an argument, when he was thinking over what happened, he was able to identify his anger and hurt-producing thoughts and rationally respond to them.

"I don't want her to withdraw, but she can. I am powerless to make her stop withdrawing, but she can. She manipulates me sometimes but not all the time. Often she is really very hurt and that is why she withdraws and cries. When she is in that state it does no good to tell her what has hurt me and what I want. It's best to wait until later."

After Sean had repeated this process of thinking things over after an argument a number of times, he started to remind himself during the argument itself that some of his thoughts were making his anger worse and that he could release these thoughts in favor of more rationally balanced thoughts.

He used the same idea to deal with his hurtful thoughts. "She does love me. There is plenty of evidence for that. Just because she withdraws doesn't mean she's abandoning me. I know that it's good to expect to be loved by Jennifer, but not to demand or require it. I am worthy of her love even though I've done things to her I'm not proud of—things that I intend to change."

In this way, Sean became ready to completely release his character defects and to make direct amends to Jennifer. He worked to modify his thoughts when he realized he was thinking in such a way as would prevent progress. He knew he was powerless to directly change his feelings, but he could take responsibility for them by taking responsibility for his thoughts and thought patterns.

The work of Step Eight is simply identifying those to whom you owe amends and becoming willing to make amends. In Troubled Couples Anonymous the focus is specifically on becoming willing to make amends to your spouse. This work is distinct from the work of the previous seven steps, but it is impossible to do until after you have completed them.

Think back for a moment to your Twelve Step work up to now. It was easy to pinpoint your spouse's character defects. But it was hard to identify your own unfulfilled needs that formed the basis of your resentment of these character defects, and harder still to let go of your intent to change your spouse.

Once you began to let go of the idea that you had to change your spouse, and you let go of your resentment against him or her one day at a time, you were able to look to God to help you fulfill your unmet needs. "Turning it over" meant giving your needs up to God and trusting Him to fulfill them. You explored the result of your unfulfilled needs when you took a fearless moral inventory. The character flaws you identified in yourself had developed within you as a result of needs left unfulfilled in childhood. When you admitted the full extent of these childhood hurts and the resultant character defects, it opened the way for healing.

You asked God to heal your hurtful memories and to provide the nurturing and love you needed. You took responsibility to parent yourself so far as these unfulfilled needs and childhood hurts were concerned. You actively confronted the destructive core beliefs and "tapes" left over from these hurtful incidents. With God's help, you undertook the healing of your inner child.

Your character defects and their destructive effects on your marriage remained. Humbly, you asked God to remove your character failings, even though you knew it would be a process to fully release them. Now it is time to become willing to make amends for the destructive effects of your character defects in the lives of other people. In this chapter you have seen two partners in a troubled marriage go through the process of becoming willing to make their amends. Specifically, the process of becoming willing entails the direct confrontation of the destructive core beliefs. These are the "tapes" that run when you fight with your spouse.

It is not easy! That is why the first seven steps concern only your issues. In an important way Step Eight concerns the very same things. When Greg became aware of the tape running in his head during his fights with Julie ("She doesn't respect me! She's saying these things to hurt me."), he realized his own unfulfilled need for respect. He wanted Julie to fulfill this need, but had to first become aware of the destructive beliefs preventing him from making progress. Once he began to confront these beliefs within himself he became less angry and more willing to make amends.

Sean took the same steps to become willing to make amends to Jennifer. Though he was deeply hurt when Jennifer abruptly cut off their arguments and refused to listen to him, he forgave her for each of the incidents where she had done that to him. He knew she would continue to cut off their arguments and refuse to listen, and he knew it would continue to hurt him. The part that hurt the most each time was the feeling of abandonment when Jennifer cut off the communication. ("She's abandoning me. She doesn't care!") He decided to work on his end of the problem as part of his Step Eight.

In the Step Guide for Step Eight you will have the opportunity to do the same work that Greg did in his marriage to Julie and Sean in his with Jennifer. Completing the Step Guide will help you remove the final obstacles to making amends to your spouse. Using the same skills you developed in Steps Four and Six, you will uncover the anger-producing thoughts you have about your spouse and the hurt which lies just below your anger.

STEP GUIDE: STEP EIGHT

Step Eight is becoming willing to make amends to your spouse. In order to become fully willing to make your amends you must first deal with your anger and hurt. The work you are about to undertake provides you with the tools to do that.

Complete the following inventory sheets in your journal. The first part has to do with identifying and rationally responding to your anger-producing thoughts. The second part exposes the hurt underneath the anger, specifically the unfulfilled need which is the basis of your hurt. Both Greg's and Sean's inventory sheets are provided as examples.

BECOMING WILLING TO MAKE AMENDS FOR YOUR CHARACTER DEFECTS

GREG

1.

> **THE CHARACTER DEFECT(S) MOST HURTFUL TO YOUR SPOUSE**
>
> Insensitivity

2.

> **YOUR WAY OF ACTING OUT THE DEFECT OF CHARACTER**
>
> "Not listening to Julie."
> "Ignoring Julie."
> "Discounting her view."

3.

> **ROOTS OF YOUR CHARACTER DEFECT**
>
> Hurtful childhood experiences: his father didn't listen to him as a child/adolescent. Hurtful experiences with Julie: Julie criticizes him in front of others at church and in business.

4.

> **FORGIVE EACH RESENTMENT**
>
> Recall his Step Six work. Forgave father for each incident he could recall of disrespect and abuse.
> Forgave Julie for each incident he could recall of disrespect.

5.

> **IDENTIFY OBSTACLES TO YOUR WILLINGNESS: Deal with your anger and hurt**
>
> Recalled hurtful incidents. Identified irrational traps and beliefs in each situation. Answered each one rationally using the work sheet, p. 66.

6.

> **IDENTIFY VIRTUE WHICH IS THE OPPOSITE OF YOUR DEFECT OF CHARACTER**
>
> Character defect = insensitivity
> Way to act out = not listening
> Positive trait = sensitivity
> Means to making amends = active listening

BECOMING WILLING TO MAKE AMENDS FOR YOUR CHARACTER DEFECTS

SEAN

1.

THE CHARACTER DEFECT(S) MOST HURTFUL TO YOUR SPOUSE

Demanding, Abusive, or Indifference/ Withdrawal

2.

YOUR WAY OF ACTING OUT THE DEFECT OF CHARACTER

"Yelling, pressing the point even after Jennifer is crying or withdrawn OR being cold, distant, withdrawn."

3.

ROOTS OF YOUR CHARACTER DEFECT

Hurtful childhood experiences: his father was emotionally unavailable when he drank. Hurtful experiences with Jennifer: Jennifer says, "enough" and emotionally abandons Sean.

4.

FORGIVE EACH RESENTMENT

Recalled his Step Six work. Forgave father for each incident he could recall of emotional abandonment.
Forgave Jennifer for each incident he could recall of withdrawal and abandonment.

5.

IDENTIFY OBSTACLES TO YOUR WILLINGNESS: Deal with your anger and hurt

Recalled hurtful incidents. Identified irrational traps and beliefs in each situation. Answered each one rationally using the work sheet, p. 66.

6.

IDENTIFY VIRTUE WHICH IS THE OPPOSITE OF YOUR DEFECT OF CHARACTER

Character Defect = demanding/abusive and indifference/withdrawal
Way to act out = pressing Jennifer OR being cold
Positive traits = esteem/respect and tenderness/intimacy
Means to making amends = feeling statements, active listening, I-statements, assertiveness.

GREG'S PART ONE: ANGER

SITUATION	HOW I FELT RATE 1–100	CORE BELIEFS/ THOUGHTS IN SITUATION	OPERATIVE CHARACTER DEFECT	RATIONAL RESPONSE	NEW FEELING AND OPPOSITE VIRTUE
"Julie criticized me again—in front of everyone at the church ministry. After, she wanted me to 'listen' to her and take her concerns 'seriously.' Her 'suggestions' are really criticisms."	Anger 85 Resent-ment 80	"She did this specifically to hurt me and 'prove her point.'" "She continually puts me down and criticizes me. She hasn't stopped and she won't stop no matter how much Twelve Step work I do!"	Assuming the worst Tendency to hold resentment Passive-Aggression	"She's angry about something. I want to know specifically what it is." "She doesn't always criticize me. Only when she's very angry about something."	Anger 40 *Don't assume the worst. Instead investigate with an open mind. Resentful 40 *Release resentment as soon as possible. *Assertively ask her to stop criticizing but don't demand.

GREG'S PART TWO: HURT

SITUATION	HOW I FELT RATE 1–100	CORE BELIEFS/ THOUGHTS IN SITUATION	OPERATIVE CHARACTER DEFECT	RATIONAL RESPONSE	NEW FEELING AND OPPOSITE VIRTUE
"Julie criticized me again—in front of everyone at the church ministry. After, she wanted me to 'listen' to her and take her concerns 'seriously.' Her 'suggestions' are really criticisms."	Humiliated 90 Disrespected/ Put down 90 Hurt 70 Hopeless 80	"She doesn't speak respectfully to me in front of others." "She doesn't respect me at all." "She doesn't love me." "She'll always be this way."	Uncaring Unaffectionate Abusive/ Demanding	"I want her to speak respectfully to me even when she's very angry at me. I know that is her character defect and her choice." "She does respect me in many ways. I want her to show it." "I know that she does love me, even though it's hard for me to believe sometimes." "People change. I want to change and grow. I want her to also."	Humiliation 30 Determination 70 *I will show caring/ affection for her and not withhold it as punishment. Disrespected 30 *Co-operation *Assertiveness I'll show love and respect even when I don't think it is given. I won't do it grudgingly, but when I feel I can cheerfully. Hopeful 30

SEAN'S PART ONE: ANGER

SITUATION	HOW I FELT RATE 1–100	CORE BELIEFS/ THOUGHTS IN SITUATION	OPERATIVE CHARACTER DEFECT	RATIONAL RESPONSE	NEW FEELING AND OPPOSITE VIRTUE
"Jennifer cut-off our fight again. She just throws up her hands and says, 'enough' and she won't talk to me."	Anger 90 Resentful 90	"She can't do this. She shouldn't do this. She manipu-lates everything in an argument and if she can't she stops and cries."	Coercion Tendency to hold resentment Passive-Aggressive	"She can do it but I don't like it. It's not that she 'shouldn't' but rather that I don't want her to. I know I cannot make her stop withdrawing. It's not always manipulation. Sometimes she is really hurt. When she's in that state it does no good to tell her what has hurt me and what I want. It's best to wait, but tell her later."	Anger 35 *Respect and an open mind. It's her decision to withdraw or not. Resentful 40 *Release resentment as much as possible. *Assertively wait but tell her later without blaming.

SEAN'S PART TWO: HURT

SITUATION	HOW I FELT RATE 1–100	CORE BELIEFS/ THOUGHTS IN SITUATION	OPERATIVE CHARACTER DEFECT	RATIONAL RESPONSE	NEW FEELING AND OPPOSITE VIRTUE
"Jennifer cut-off our fight again. She just throws up her hands and says, 'enough' and she won't talk to me."	Abandoned 90 Uncared for 90 Unloved 90 Hurt 90 Depressed 75	"She doesn't care enough to stick in our argument." "She emotionally withdraws and abandons me." "She doesn't love me and never has." "I'm not worthy of her love anyway. How can I expect it after what I've done to her?"	Coercion Abusive/ Demand-ing Or Indiffer-ence/ Withdrawal	"She does love me. There's plenty of evidence for that. Just because she withdraws in an argument doesn't mean she's abandoning me altogether." "I know she loves me and I expect it, but I don't demand or require it. I am worthy of her love even though I have done things I'm not proud of."	Uncared for 30 Abandoned 30 *Release *Detachment *Respect I won't try to force my way in when she shuts me out. I will "knock on the door." Loved 30 Hopeful 30 *I won't withdraw when she withdraws or force my way in. I will show affection when she's ready.

9

MAKING AMENDS

> **STEP NINE: MADE DIRECT AMENDS TO SUCH PEO-**
> **PLE WHEREVER POSSIBLE, EXCEPT WHEN TO DO**
> **SO WOULD INJURE THEM OR OTHERS.**

This is the moment you have been waiting for. Trying to make amends for what they have done wrong is where most people begin to work on healing their troubled marriage. But without first making themselves ready mentally, emotionally, and spiritually, they frequently fall into the same old controlling habits as before. Since you have taken the time to renew yourself spiritually, and become more alert to your role in the marriage and how your own character defects have harmed your spouse, you are ready to make amends. Taking responsibility for setting these wrongs right is a constructive action you can take on behalf of your marriage, but also on your own behalf. Making amends restores integrity to your actions and builds self-esteem.

Making amends is where you begin to re-establish the foundation of your relationship with your spouse, which is trust. Present yourself to your partner in a humble way and acknowledge what you have discovered: how your character defects have hurt your growth in intimacy as a couple. Naturally, making amends will include people other than your wife or husband. Here, though, we will focus solely on making amends to your spouse.

There are two parts to making amends, both equally important. The first part is making amends indirectly. The second part is making direct amends. Indirect amends include all the work you are doing to understand and have God remove your own character defects, including developing the corresponding virtues to each. Indirect amends includes forming good communication skills in order to express yourself clearly and sincerely. Indirect amends includes the willingness to take inventory of yourself, admit your failings when they occur, and seek the healing necessary. Direct amends are made by a careful inventory of wrongs done that you share with your spouse and ask forgiveness for.

INDIRECT AMENDS

The best preparation for direct amends is by making indirect amends a priority in your life. The most important part of your recovery program is discovering your own character defects and the corresponding virtues that will actually fulfill your needs. Take a moment now to recall those character flaws that hurt your spouse the most. Recall, also, the character defects and actions of your spouse that continue to hurt you. The Marital Needs Inventory includes a list of the areas in which you must work to make indirect amends, and the areas you will have to ask your spouse to work on.

MARITAL NEEDS INVENTORY

ITEMS	CHARACTER DEFECTS	NEEDS	VIRTUES
1, 2	Indifference/Withdrawal	Affection	Intimacy/Tenderness
3, 4	Degradation/Abusiveness	Respect	Admiration/Esteem
5, 6	Inadequacy/Incompetency	Skill	Competency/Achievement
7, 8	Distortion/Insensitivity	Understanding	Empathy/Sensitivity
9, 10	Aggressiveness/Coercion	Power & Influence	Cooperation/Inspiration
11, 12	Wastefulness/Poverty	Economic Well-being	Productivity/Resourcefulness
13, 14	Anxiety/Irritability	Personal Well-being	Happiness/Satisfaction
15, 16	Selfishness/Infidelity	Responsibility	Authenticity/Commitment
17, 18	Self-absorption/Alienation	Sexual Fulfillment	Enjoyment/Integration
19, 20	Abusiveness/Ineffectiveness	Parenting	Nurturance/Effectiveness

It is important to know which character defect is most hurtful to your spouse. Clear communication is necessary to determine this, as well as (and just as important) when, in your partner's view, your actions reflect this particular character defect.

COMMUNICATION

The communication between you and your spouse doubtless became more and more inadequate as your marriage problems progressed. Constant conflict makes honest sharing of feelings impossible. As long as you considered yourself locked in battle with the enemy, any talking you have done has been either defensive or offensive. Now is the time to clear up communication problems, as this is the primary instrument of re-engagement.

Communication is the way you deal with your character defects and those of your spouse. Communication is the vehicle in which you take responsibility for your character defects and through which you ask your spouse to take responsibility for his or her character defects.

The reliance on God for healing and direction makes it possible to enter into discussion freely and without fear of losing something or having to win something. The key to progress is communicating the truth, what you really think and feel. From God you receive the strength to grant forgiveness, to release your spouse from the emotional and spiritual debt he or she owes you. Releasing your own character defects to God's care changes your thoughts about your spouse. Deeply ingrained thoughts and perceptions give way to more accurate and empathetic views. You have come to see your marriage partner as having both strengths and weaknesses. More importantly, with God's help you are becoming more accepting of them as well.

In trying to really share with your spouse what is on your mind and heart, you take the risk of being hurt again. It has happened before. Your partner will be suspicious of any new attempt. He or she will be doubtful that it is going to work or that you are sincere, which is understandable because of the climate that has existed between you. It is important to humbly acknowledge the situation as it really stands. It should not change your mind, however, about what you have resolved to do.

FIGHTING TO SOLVE PROBLEMS

Fighting with your spouse up until now has probably been destructive to your relationship. A healthy marriage includes arguments, disagreements, and blowing off steam. It is possible to fight and actually resolve issues. This type of fighting means fighting fair[1] and exercising certain skills. It also involves respect for your spouse. Below are two basic skills useful in communicating during conflict.

ACTIVE LISTENING

Active listening is a communication tool that helps you understand clearly what your spouse is trying to tell you. There are two parts to the skill. First, you restate the message your partner gives you with emphasis on how he or she feels about it. The second part is waiting for your spouse to tell you if you have accurately reflected his or her sentiments.

A simple way to begin using the active listening skill is to use the words, "What I hear you saying is . . ." The statement may seem simplistic but it will help you to start. When you use active listening, put the phrase in your own words. For example, "From what you're saying . . ." or "From your point of view, you feel . . ." Create phrases that are honest and sincere for you.

As with any skill, active listening takes practice. Do not expect to be able to restate the feelings or opinions of your spouse correctly each time. Be ready to be corrected by your spouse. He or she will probably restate what was said if you do not accurately restate the meaning. Your spouse may not directly state what he or she really wants to say the first time. By repeating what you understand, you give your spouse the opportunity to modify his or her statement to convey more accurately what he or she is really thinking and feeling.

Active listening is not as easy as it sounds. In the middle of an argument it is difficult to restate what your spouse is feeling. Try using this skill when there is no argument at first. When you succeed you will have achieved accurate empathy. That is, you will know as much as it is humanly possible about what your spouse is thinking and feeling about a given issue.

Many partners in troubled marriages think they already know what their partner is thinking and feeling without having to ask. This is known as "mind reading." It leads to misunderstandings and the sense of being taken for granted. Active listening allows you to use the legitimate knowledge you have about your spouse, rather than simply trying to guess what your partner is thinking.

Another obstacle that hinders active listening is your own emotions, such as anger or hurt. Greg and Julie, who were introduced in the previous chapter, had difficulty listening to each other. Greg worked hard to change the way he thought about Julie, particularly while they were arguing. His thoughts were fueling his anger. When he tried to use active listening he found that he could not do it. He was too angry to accurately perceive what Julie was saying or feeling.

After several incidents, Greg confronted his thoughts about Julie. When he found himself thinking, "She doesn't respect me," he responded, "At times she does show me respect, and I know she respects me in many ways. Right now, she is angry. However, I want her to speak to me courteously even when she is angry. I understand this is hard for her. It is one of her character defects."

After his own anger subsided, Greg could inquire about what it was that Julie was making herself angry over. He phrased his question in words like, "You're angry at me because you believe I never listen to your ideas." This effectively was an invitation to Julie to speak openly. It told her he really wanted to understand her point of view.

Greg had to be in touch with his own anger and deal with it honestly before active listening could be used effectively. He also had to understand Julie's weaknesses. In this way he began to modify the defensive habits that prevented them from effectively communicating with each other and resolving problems.

THE "I FEEL" STATEMENT

A second tool to help you in communicating well during an argument is to put your words in the form of an "I feel" statement. This forces you to be honest about your emotions. Your spouse does not cause you to feel a certain way. Feelings are your response to your interpretation of events. Framing your words in an "I feel" statement helps you to take responsibility for your emotions and express your feelings more honestly. "I feel" statements enable you to express your feelings without blaming your spouse for anything. For example, "I feel angry when I believe you are putting me down in front of others," in place of, "You *make* me angry when *you put me down* in front of others."

How could Greg express his frustration without making Julie angrier? First, it took a lot of courage to express his feelings at all. He was "gun shy" about how Julie would take what he said. Releasing past hurts and changing his own anger-producing thoughts helped give him the confidence to try.

In the same way he changed his inner thoughts, Greg tried to change his usual style of communicating with Julie. He often used inflammatory and accusatory statements. For example, "You never speak respectfully to me in front of other people. You just barge in with your cockamamie ideas!" Then he would wonder why Julie became so defensive.

Again, when he tried to modify his communication with Julie he found more anger-producing thoughts blocked his path. "Why should I have to pick and choose my words so carefully so as not to offend her? What about *my* feelings?"

He became more and more angry until he caught himself and rationally responded, "I don't *have* to choose my words carefully, but I *want* to so that I will clearly communicate my feelings and what I want her to do." Greg chose to rephrase his statements because it helped him to better make his point. It suited his desire to build his marriage. Deep down inside, he sincerely wanted to resolve these issues rather than hurt either Julie or himself.

Greg modified his pattern of communication. Before an argument broke out he made statements like the following: "I feel frustrated. I know you respect me, so I want to know how you've become so angry that you ended up criticizing me in front of our friends."

Formulating his statement, Greg tried to take responsibility for his own thoughts and feelings while expressing them to Julie. He avoided indicting her for her shortcomings, even though he wanted to tell her exactly what she was doing wrong. Greg was a counselor himself. He worked in a church and gave other people advice. Consequently, he thought he knew exactly what she should do. "I'm head of this family. I should be able to lead my wife in spiritual matters."

Greg came to realize the way to lead his family was by example, not just by pointing out errors. Although in his capacity as a church minister he had a license and a responsibility to direct and counsel others, at home this was not his role. Within a few months of concerted effort, Greg made significant progress modifying his thought patterns and style of communication. He successfully "bit his tongue" in the middle of accusatory statements directed to hurt Julie and replaced them with "I feel" statements. Julie responded positively to Greg's adaptations and responded with less anger. She realized he was honestly trying to hear what she had to say.

There are two other principles to keep in mind during this amends making period. The first principle is *assertiveness* and the second is *honesty*. These are related to each other and to the communication skills just described.

ASSERTIVENESS

Assertiveness is defined as *stating what you need and what you want*. As such, assertiveness has to do with asking, rather than demanding, that your spouse work on his or her character flaws and actions which are most hurtful to you. We have already addressed the importance of assertively refusing to submit to abuse of any type, physical, sexual, or otherwise. Assertiveness as a principle of communication is important in making indirect amends. Anyone who identified Passive/ Aggressiveness as a character defect in their moral inventory will use assertiveness as the remedy.

Assertiveness in marriage means frankly telling your partner what you need and what you want from him or her in such a way that you build your relationship. Assertiveness is distinct from aggressiveness in that there is no intent to fulfill your need or want by force or at your spouse's expense.

Susan and Bob had explosive fights. Whenever Susan attempted to confront Bob she would receive some type of criticism in return. There were plenty of serious issues that needed to be resolved between them, but most often they argued over frustrating petty annoyances. Even these, Susan felt, Bob twisted around so that she was to blame for everything.

Susan thought carefully about making indirect amends and being assertive. She decided instead of sulking over the dismal state of their bedroom—due to Bob's sloppiness—she would do something. In times past she would simply add this to her "nag list" though she knew it was ineffective to nag and that this was one of her character defects. She would say, "You always leave your clothes all over the floor!"

Bob would turn it around and say, "If you'd do the laundry more often there wouldn't be so many clothes around, now would there?"

She decided to take action and communicate assertively. She used an "I feel" statement first: "I would really appreciate it if you would put your dirty clothes in the hamper in the morning." Then she decided only the clothes that had been placed in the hamper would be washed and not those left around their bedroom. When she finally got disgusted with the appearance of the bedroom she would place the clothes in the hamper when she wanted to—often after the laundry was already done. She did not nag nor mention the issue again. She stated plainly what she wanted but did not attempt to force Bob into doing what she wanted him to do. When Bob complained that his favorite clothes were still dirty, Susan repeated her request. She knew in the long run this assertive but quiet approach would work better than nagging him.

HONESTY

"It's an honest program." In Troubled Couples Anonymous honesty is both a virtue and an important communication principle. Honesty is distinguished from "brutal honesty." Brutal honesty, by mistake or design, is hurtful to your partner. As Step Nine suggests, we are not to hurt others in the name of honesty. Share your thoughts and opinions with your spouse, even though he or she may disagree. That is part of intimacy. Sharing a thought or opinion delicately is a skill which many partners in troubled marriages have ceased to practice. In Troubled Couples Anonymous, you are encouraged to share your innermost thoughts and feelings with your spouse in a way that will strengthen your relationship. This takes both skill and courage.

If it is hard to say, it is probably important to say. In a troubled marriage there are resentments which have been around so long they seem to have ceased being resentments. How can you resent something that seems always to have been true in your relationship? At first you resent it. Then you grow to accept it or become resigned to it, and the resentment seems to be gone. In Step One you were asked to identify the one or two character defects in your spouse which hurt you the most. You were also asked to look squarely at your habit of resentment surrounding these character defects and begin to abstain from the habit of resentment. To do this it was necessary to stop obsessing about your spouse and the character defects that hurt you, focusing on yourself rather than your partner. With Step Nine, you are asked to re-engage your spouse in this painful area—to honestly admit your hurt and your part in perpetuating the problem. You are equipped to do this because of your moral inventory, and your work in healing of memories and forgiveness. It is still difficult, however, because honesty is often misunderstood.

Recall again Julie and Greg. Greg felt hurt when Julie spoke directly about his character defect (that he did not seem to really listen to her). Because Julie spoke out of her hurt and anger, her complaint came out as biting criticism.

"I'm just being honest with him. I can't stand it when he shuts me out and stops taking me seriously."

Julie thought she was just being honest. But what she was saying perpetuated the problems between them. When she stopped being brutally honest with Greg and began being truly honest with herself, she decided to stop her pattern of accusatory "You" statements and to begin using honest "I feel" statements.

This was hard work. Julie naturally tended to point out Greg's problem with "tuning her out." She found herself literally biting her tongue to keep from doing it. The "I feel" statements felt artificial at first because of her anger. It also felt risky because under her anger Julie felt hurt. Admitting her hurt to Greg meant she was vulnerable to be hurt again.

Honesty in communication reopens the wounds that denial and controlling behavior led you to believe were healed. Honesty does not reopen the wound permanently, however. The right dose of honesty and confrontation of the problem puts you in touch with the work that remains to be done. The wounds are reopened only enough to foster a more complete healing. For Julie, using "I feel" statements and being honest with herself meant feeling vulnerable before Greg. She honestly admitted to herself that she was only ready to trust him a little. She had to get back in touch with her original decision to forgive him and renew it each day. This meant continuing to take responsibility for her own role in the marriage. Only then could she begin to make indirect amends by changing her communication from disrespectful "You" statements to more assertive and respectful "I feel" statements. She became ready in this way to make direct amends.

COMMUNICATION

ACTIVE LISTENING
   "What I hear you saying is . . ."
   Tune into what your partner really feels.

"I FEEL" STATEMENT
   Take responsibility for your emotions and express them more
   directly.

ASSERTIVENESS
   State what you need and what you want.

HONESTY
   Say it, but say it diplomatically. Honesty can build your intimacy.
   Brutal honesty can hurt your partner and cause resentment.

DIRECT AMENDS

This may well be the most difficult part of your Twelve Step program. It is never easy to admit when you are wrong. The admission you are to make here is directly to your spouse. The acquired false self will balk at the very notion of admitting to the "enemy" that you have done anything wrong. Made mistakes? Of course—doesn't everyone? But to take responsibility and ask forgiveness for these wrongs? How can you face your partner with such an admission? It seems like giving your very self away without receiving anything in return.

Remember the game, "I'll apologize; but *only* if you will!" The time has come to apologize unconditionally. Period. You have done your Twelve Step work thoroughly until now, so your apology will not be hollow. It will ring true and sincere. It will be an act of self-giving on par with the events of your wedding day. On that day you gave yourself to your spouse for better or worse, richer or poorer, in sickness and in health, for as long as you both live. That type of giving has been missing in your marriage for a long time. It is time to bring it back.

When you take full responsibility for your part in rebuilding your marriage it is a joyful event. It is in a real sense remarrying your partner. You are in effect saying, "I would do it all over again. Even knowing what I know now, I would marry my husband or wife all over again because I love him or her. I don't blame my partner for what I have put myself through."

If you are not ready to make these words your own then do not attempt to make your direct amends now. Go back and work the first eight steps more thoroughly. Remember that the Twelve Steps are a process for recovery and you are on your own timetable—no one else's. You may take as much time as you need to get ready for each step. When you define your wrongs and promise to make them right you are giving away your bargaining position. Any negotiation that takes place after the event of direct amends automatically becomes negotiation in good faith. There is no turning back. It is a full commitment.

ASKING FORGIVENESS

Granting forgiveness to your spouse was a part of preparing to have God remove your character defects. Forgiveness in the context of Step Six meant canceling the debt you held over your spouse for some hurt he or she caused you. Step Nine is about obtaining forgiveness. Making direct amends to your spouse means asking for forgiveness and offering to make up for the damage you have done as best you can. Of course, you cannot completely repair the damage done. It is up to your spouse to grant you forgiveness. It is a free choice only he or she can make. Your part is to do your best to make it easier for your partner to forgive by making amends.

It is especially difficult to make direct amends to your spouse when infidelity is the offense. Just the reference to this breach of trust opens old wounds. There clearly is no way to make up for it. In cases where unfaithfulness is suspected by your spouse but not confirmed, choose your words carefully so as to not inadvertently hurt your spouse while trying to apologize. There is no need to go into details or specific incidents. Depending on the circumstances, the admission of past wrongs and promise of future fidelity should emphasize your commitment and love for your partner. Even when details are known to both of you it is important to emphasize your renewed commitment to the marriage. Guilt feelings and an earnest desire to make up for the past may prompt you to go into details. This may make you feel better, but it can adversely affect your spouse. Review this with your sponsor beforehand if you have some doubt as to what to say.

Whatever the area of wrongdoing, it is best to emphasize the nature of your responsibility, how you failed, and that you seek forgiveness. There is no need to glamorize it; just tell it like it is. The reason for admitting your wrongs is to ask your partner's forgiveness. You own up to your character defects and make a promise to work to improve these areas of your life. By this stage the recovery work you have been doing will encourage your husband or wife to recognize your apology as sincere.

There is no guarantee, however. Making direct amends is a risk. Your spouse may doubt your sincerity. If this is the case, do not be discouraged. Try not to argue or cajole your spouse into accepting your apology. Instead, humbly accept the fact that your spouse needs more time and perhaps more evidence in order to trust you again in these areas. Trust can be rebuilt. It takes time and work. Even if your spouse seems unwilling to allow this to happen, if you do your part well, it will exert positive pressure on him or her. Although you cannot force forgiveness and trust, you can influence your partner's free choice through honesty and candor.

MAKING DIRECT AMENDS

Julie found honesty with Greg did not mean openly criticizing him. Real honesty was far more risky. It involved admitting to herself just how hurt she felt. Underneath her anger she was really hurt that he did not listen to her. Her anger was a kind of shield against being hurt again—or at least feeling the hurt.

When she decided to make indirect amends to Greg she changed her accusatory language to "I feel" statements. This forced her to be more honest with herself and with Greg. All she needed to say was the truth about how angry or hurt she was. She did not have to justify her feeling by blaming him or accusing him of something.

Julie also decided to make direct amends to Greg. She could be stubborn and headstrong. She knew what hurt him most was when she criticized him in front of their friends and church members. She also had enough insight into her own character defect to know she tended to criticize him most intensively after he had disregarded her opinion about something important. It also happened when he became intensely interested in the business or his church work. She realized she acted out her character defect most frequently when she felt victimized by what she considered his character defect, his insensitivity toward her. Direct amends meant freely acknowledging this habit and making a sincere promise to work on changing this pattern of behavior. She would henceforth try her best not to exact revenge when she felt ignored. Instead, she would tell Greg how she felt.

Although there were other character weaknesses she knew she must work on, Julie knew she could focus on only one thing at a time. When she prepared her Step Nine she made sure to acknowledge all these areas that had been hurtful to Greg. She made it clear to him that she had targeted this tendency to criticize him in front of others as the first change she planned to make.

She carefully prepared the wording she would use in taking Step Nine. She knew by bringing up the topic she would be tempted to shift the blame onto Greg. So, she not only prepared the precise wording she would use but she also talked herself through the situation by rehearsing it in her mind.

Julie believed she knew Greg well enough to be able to predict his reaction to her confession. She knew he would avoid the direct appearance of saying, "I told you I was right and you were wrong all along." However, he would probably take her Step Nine gesture as a confirmation that he was right and that he had nothing of any consequence to work on himself.

This was a great concern to Julie. She did not want to give Greg the impression that the way he ignored her and discounted her opinions and feelings was all right with her. Exactly the opposite was true. She knew from her work in the program that her admission of faults did not mean she had given up her desire for Greg to work on his faults. But the time to address Greg's faults was not while making amends for her own wrongdoing. It was her amends that she was focusing on at this moment.

The rational thinking and communication skills she had learned were important for framing the issues correctly. Referring to her own faults without reference to Greg's seemed unfair, as though she was accepting full blame for their marriage problems. She answered herself by saying full admission for her character defect of criticizing Greg in front of others is just that: full admission of her responsibility. She was not accepting blame for all their marriage problems. She would claim full responsibility for her actions, but no more. To cross the line and accept more would not accomplish anything good.

The more Julie prepared to make direct amends, the unfinished work of making indirect amends came into sharper focus. If she were really going to surrender her only weapon in forcing Greg to listen to her and notice her, she needed another more effective tool for getting through to him. Being assertive and honest in her communication about her feelings was the way she would go. Without a commitment to this new way, when times got rough, Julie knew she would fall back on old destructive habits. In this way, assertiveness—standing up for herself at those times she felt she was being ignored—was an essential part of her Step Nine amends-making process. Committing herself to responsibility and amends making for her weaknesses was also a commitment to her relationship with Greg. She was trusting him with her true thoughts and feelings, hoping he would understand.

STEP GUIDE: STEP NINE

Step nine is making amends to your partner. There are two parts to the amends-making process: indirect amends and direct amends.

PART ONE: PREPARATION

Review the Marital Needs Inventory Chart on page 162. Use the chart and your Step Four inventory to clearly identify the character defects and behaviors which have hurt your spouse the most. Indirect amends include your actions and efforts to take responsibility for the ways you have hurt your spouse. You will indirectly offer amends by changing what you do. The degree to which you are successful will lend credibility to your direct amends when you verbally ask your partner's forgiveness and offer direct reparation.

Examine the Destructive Cycle chart on page 180. It illustrates the way Julie's and Greg's character defects feed into one another and build resentment. Julie's unfulfilled need for understanding from Greg is the basis of her resentment toward him. She desperately wants Greg to listen to her and understand her. Julie's character defect is the tendency to verbally abuse and degrade Greg. The most hurtful way she acts out her character defect toward Greg is when she degrades and criticizes him in front of their friends. This, in turn, feeds into Greg's unfulfilled need for respect from Julie. His resentment builds and he ends up acting out his character defect of insensitivity and passive aggressiveness by ignoring Julie, not listening to her, and discounting the value of her opinions. She, in turn, feels resentful and misunderstood, completing the cycle.

In your journal answer the following questions:

1. What is your spouse's chief character defect?

2. How does your spouse act it out to hurt you?

3. What is your unfulfilled need (which forms the basis of your resentment)?

4. What is your chief character defect?

5. What is your way of acting it out—the way which is most hurtful to your spouse?

6. What is your spouse's unfulfilled need?

You may not be able to pinpoint each answer exactly, but make your best attempt. Since you now have a clearer idea of your partner's unfulfilled need and the way your character defect has hurt him or her, you also have the information you need to make indirect and direct amends.

Examine How Making Amends Interrupts the Destructive Cycle and Builds a Positive Cycle chart on page 181. It illustrates the way Julie and Greg each took responsibility for their character defects and hurtful actions. Julie became aware of her unfulfilled need for understanding and began to take responsibility for her need by abstaining from her way of acting out her character defect (verbally abusing and criticizing Greg). She made indirect amends by using "I" statements to clearly state her feelings, views, and opinions to make it easier for Greg to understand her. It was hard work for Julie to do this because of her anger toward Greg and her habitual way of expressing her anger by criticizing him. Julie's indirect amends to Greg served as a kind of amends to herself. She began to more effectively communicate her feelings, needs, and wants.

Julie made direct amends by taking responsibility for criticizing Greg in front of their friends. She apologized and asked forgiveness verbally and directly. She promised to stop. She looked for opportunities to express admiration and respect for Greg in front of their friends.

Greg, for his part, became aware of his unfulfilled need for respect and his way of acting out against Julie (ignoring her, not listening to her). He made indirect amends to Julie and to himself by assertively expressing that he felt disrespected and criticized. This was hard for Greg because it required taking a risk. His old way was far safer; say nothing, just turn off and stop listening. He did his best to express his feelings and let go of Julie's response.

Greg made direct amends by taking responsibility for ignoring Julie and discounting her opinion. He verbally and directly asked Julie's forgiveness. He promised to listen to Julie even at times when he did not feel like it. He practiced active listening to understand Julie's feelings and opinions better.

In your journal answer the following questions:

1. What are your unfulfilled needs?

2. How will you take responsibility for your needs and make indirect amends to your partner and yourself?

3. How will you take responsibility for your hurtful actions toward your partner? How will you make direct amends to your partner? What actions can you take that directly make amends for your past hurtful actions by directly addressing your partner's unfulfilled need?

4. What are your partner's unfulfilled needs?

5. What form of indirect amends would you like to see your partner make?

6. What form of direct amends would you like to see your partner make?

PART TWO: MAKING AMENDS

1. Indirect amends

Practice the actions and communication skills you have decided are part of your indirect amends. Remember, indirect amends are the way you take responsibility for your own needs.

a) First abstain from the specific behaviors which are your way of acting out your character defect and retaliating against your partner when you feel hurt.

b) Form a plan of action to fulfill your own need. Are there actions you can take to satisfy your need without hurting your partner? For example, Julie planned time with a close friend to address her need for someone to listen. Her intention was not to replace Greg, but to not rely on Greg exclusively to fulfill her need for empathy and support.

c) Make indirect amends by practicing applicable rational thinking and communication skills. Review the list of irrational traps and rational responses (pp. 144–146) and the chart of communication skills (p. 171). Target the two or three most important skills for you to work on.

2. Direct Amends

This may be the hardest individual task in your Twelve Step program. You will verbally and directly take responsibility for the ways you have hurt your partner both deliberately and inadvertently. You will ask forgiveness. You will promise to do better. All of this will be done without reference to the ways in which your spouse has hurt you.

a) Write your direct amends down word-for-word exactly as you plan to say it. Be brief and to-the-point. Reread *Asking Forgiveness* (pp. 172–173).

b) Read your direct amends over a few days after you have written it. If you feel it is necessary, go over it with your sponsor. Be careful to eliminate any implication of blame toward your spouse for your actions.

c) Read your direct amends to your partner. Explain that the reason you are reading your direct amends is that you have taken time to prepare what you have to say and you want to be sure to include everything. Offer to fully discuss the issues after you have finished presenting your direct amends.

d) Suggested outline:

1) "I want to fully admit my responsibility for the ways I have hurt you in the past. I know you have felt hurt and angry about the way I have been _____ (fill in your chief character defect)."

2) "I am sorry for the many ways this fault of mine has hurt you. I plan to make direct amends and reparation to you by _____ (fill in your direct actions which can help fulfill your partner's unfulfilled need). I know this doesn't make up for the past, but it's one way I can show that I am sincerely sorry."

3) "I will take responsibility for my hurt feelings and anger by directly telling you from now on. I will not retaliate against you by trying to hurt you back if I feel hurt. I will tell you what I want and what I need instead of trying to force you to do what I want."
4) "Please forgive me."

THE DESTRUCTIVE CYCLE

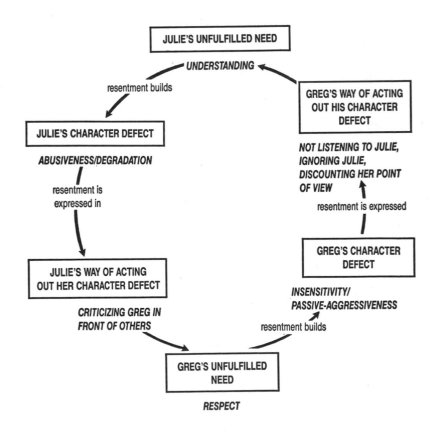

HOW MAKING AMENDS INTERRUPTS THE DESTRUCTIVE CYCLE AND BUILDS A POSITIVE CYCLE

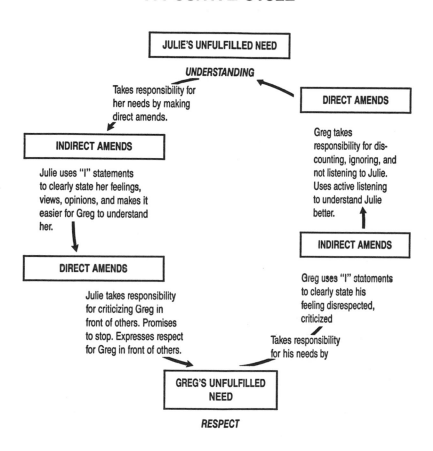

JULIE'S UNFULFILLED NEED

UNDERSTANDING

Takes responsibility for her needs by making direct amends.

DIRECT AMENDS

Greg takes responsibility for discounting, ignoring, and not listening to Julie. Uses active listening to understand Julie better.

INDIRECT AMENDS

Julie uses "I" statements to clearly state her feelings, views, opinions, and makes it easier for Greg to understand her.

INDIRECT AMENDS

Greg uses "I" statements to clearly state his feeling disrespected, criticized

DIRECT AMENDS

Julie takes responsibility for criticizing Greg in front of others. Promises to stop. Expresses respect for Greg in front of others.

Takes responsibility for his needs by

GREG'S UNFULFILLED NEED

RESPECT

$$\boxed{10}$$

PERSEVERANCE

STEP TEN: WE CONTINUED TO TAKE PERSONAL INVENTORY AND WHEN WE WERE WRONG, PROMPTLY ADMITTED IT.

Honesty and acceptance of the strengths and weaknesses of your marriage are a way of life for you now that you are integrating these twelve steps. The power to do this comes from within you in association with your Higher Power. Accepting complete responsibility for your actions, refusing to shift blame to others, and making amends where needed frees you and brings sanity and serenity to your life.

These twelve steps enable you to shape the direction of your life and marriage rather than be controlled by pride, irrational thinking, games, and so on. You are forming new ways of thinking and acting. You have made some clear progress in discovering the true nature of your marriage difficulties and the solid basis upon which to renew the relationship. Be grateful for the healing achieved so far. The rest of the journey will come in time through perseverance.

PERSONAL INVENTORY

Conflict in your marriage is natural and unavoidable. Fighting is not what makes a marriage troubled, it is whether or not it leads to constructive resolution. A good argument can be healthy for growing intimacy and honest communication. Constructive fighting is a skill partners working a Twelve Step program can learn like any other skill.[1] The work you have done thus far makes constructive fighting possible in your marriage. If you keep working the principles of your program your arguments won't get stuck. You will be able to talk about issues rather than personalities, and you won't be carrying resentments or trying to dodge responsibility.

Step Ten helps you to maintain the self-awareness necessary to head off problems that threaten your marriage. You will want to be sure resentment does not get a foothold in your marriage again. One way of monitoring your progress is a personal inventory. This is an examination of your needs and wishes, your motivations and strategies, in preparation for approaching your partner with any grievance or problem. The background anger and resentment you have painstakingly uprooted from your relationship can take hold again unless you stay alert to what is going on inside of you. Taking personal inventory, improving your spiritual attentiveness to yourself and others, should become as much a part of your life as eating, sleeping, and breathing. Here are some things to keep in mind when taking a personal inventory.

When should you take a personal inventory? When anger remains unexpressed and threatens to turn into resentment. The well-practiced tendency for most partners in a troubled marriage is to focus on their spouse's character defects. The same old thoughts—and some new ones—crop up quite readily. These thoughts go something like:

> "Leopards don't change their spots. We're right back where we started."
> "Who am I kidding? My spouse hasn't changed at all! It's the same old thing."
> "I've been fooling myself thinking we've made any progress. I might as well give up."

Your anger and irritation with your spouse grow to the point that you begin to think no progress has been made at all. You may try to talk it out. You may approach the problem as you would have before adopting the Twelve Steps. You may fall back into the old pattern of destructive fighting. But after the fight, you are left with the same lingering anger that easily turns to resentment. Should this happen, the remedy is already built into the Twelve Steps.

When resentment threatens to re-emerge, remember the work you have been doing. Focus on your partner's character defect identified in Step One. It may be the same or it may take a slightly different form. The character trait in your partner which hurts you the most is also the one that reveals the most about you. After all, your partner is a kind of mirror in which your own character defects are seen most clearly. As you have learned, however, it is far easier to see your spouse's faults than your own part in perpetuating the problem.

With your partner's character defect firmly in mind, your program becomes clear. Stay in touch with your anger, your hurt, and the unfulfilled need which forms the basis for your anger and hurt. Again, acknowledge your powerlessness over your spouse and his or her character defect. Release the responsibility for change to God and to your partner.

The most effective way to influence your partner is by acceptance of him or her as a person, including his or her weaknesses. As you know, total acceptance does not mean that you condone your partner's character defects or behavior. Acceptance simply reflects your love and commitment to your partner.

Next, dig deeper. Your trust in God strengthens you to get to the heart of the matter. Find out what is really behind your anger and hurt. Which of your needs or wants remains unfulfilled? How would you want your partner to fulfill this need? The fact that you cannot control your spouse is frustrating because you believe you are missing something. If your partner does change this defect, what benefit do you believe will come to you? Why is this bothering you now? Could this be signaling another important issue to be dealt with?

Call to mind the history of this particular conflict with your spouse. There is a grain of truth in most irrational thoughts. When that grain is extracted from the emotions and struggle for control, it usually sheds some light on the best course of action. For example:

"My spouse hasn't completely changed; basic personality usually doesn't. However, this does not mean that there's been no improvement. We have made some improvement on specific issues, even if it is less improvement than I would have wanted by now."

"Giving up is a course of action which I have considered and rejected. I decided to work a Twelve Step program because I believe it could help. The progress I have made in my personal Twelve Step program is real and undeniable. The only program I can work is my own."

The best course of action here is perseverance. When you respond to your self-talk about the state of your marriage rationally and humbly, you stay on course toward healing your marriage. Your decisions are chosen freely and based in love rather than in acquiring power over your spouse.

Forgiveness is another part of a personal inventory. If you are going to maintain an edge against resentment the regular release of any debts held against your partner is necessary. Remember, forgiveness is not automatic trust. You know your spouse will act out his or her character defect again and again. The character defect or behavior may not be acceptable but your partner as a human being is acceptable and lovable. To keep resentment from destroying YOUR life it is important to keep this distinction in mind.

Forgiveness cancels the debt you feel another owes you. It is healthier to forgive than to harbor resentment. Amends may need to be made by your spouse. That is part of his or her program, not yours. Your part is to forgive and to release as much resentment as you can today. That release opens your heart and mind to receive the good things to come.

The things that bother you about your spouse may, in reality, have nothing to do with your partner. Perhaps more inner healing is needed within yourself. In taking a personal inventory, review your attention to prayer, meditation, and response to God's will for you. The progress you have made enables you to tackle a deeper, more important challenge to love and intimacy within yourself. Embrace this and once again trust in your Higher Power.

A good personal inventory will yield awareness of unfulfilled needs or desires. The more important the need, the more panicked your reaction. Once again, you know what you must do. God knows your need and can provide for your need. He knows you are needy and sometimes powerless to obtain what you need. Release that to the care of God. Let go of the panic and replace it with faith. This will bring you serenity even in conflict or uncertainty.

A more difficult but important question to ask is how have you inadvertently perpetuated the problem? How have you enabled your spouse to continue acting out his or her character defect? How have you made it easier for your partner to stay unhealthy? Your own character weaknesses come into play with your spouse's. Which character defects do you act out in retaliation for your spouse's? If you are going to be thorough in your inventory, you have to ask yourself how your own shortcomings have gotten the better of you.

A spot inventory is the most powerful tool for keeping your program on track. Once you have identified one problem that is your direct responsibility you have clear direction again. The second part of Step Ten states, ". . . and when we were wrong promptly admitted it." This suggests an application of Step Nine: making amends. As soon as you become aware of something you are doing to harm your marriage, you humbly acknowledge it and try to repair any damage. As with your original Step Nine work, it will be difficult to admit your wrongs without reference to your partner's wrongs. Yet it is the most effective thing to do.

MAKE A PLAN

Once you identify an issue you want to discuss with your spouse, your course of action will become clear. Any behaviors that result from your character defect will have to be eliminated. Attitudes or behaviors that enable your spouse to maintain his or her character defects will have to be eliminated as well.

Abstaining from behaviors is only the first part of your plan, however. There are three other areas you will want to include in your plan: 1) improve your weakest communication skills; 2) structure the confrontation or intervention in order to make it easier for your spouse to accept his or her responsibility; and 3) plan selected assertive communication.

Before you confront your spouse with a grievance, consider the four basic communication skills discussed in a previous chapter: Active Listening, "I feel" Statements, Assertiveness, and Honesty. Which of these four is most applicable to the present situation? Again, your own character defect is the key for recognizing what is missing. For example, if your partner seems to be hurt by the things you say, and you have identified sensitivity as a trait you want to work on, Active Listening may be the communication technique you will want to concentrate on. Plan for success by strengthening your weakest areas and maximizing your strengths. Review these four skills outlined in Step Nine.

Once you have determined what needs to be said, consider how you will say it. Structure the presentation so as to make it easier for your partner to take his or her share of responsibility for the problem. This will require patience because, like most people, your spouse will resist any blame and become defensive, at least to some degree. Expect this and plan for it. Your goal is not to "fix" your partner, but to challenge your spouse with a problem and achieve some positive response.

Jack was a recovering alcoholic who had difficulty following through on promises made to his wife, Linda. Linda was exasperated with him. She worked her Twelve Step program diligently. She tried her best to refrain from nagging Jack, but it wasn't easy. If she didn't nag, Jack wouldn't follow through with what he had agreed to do.

Linda determined her course of action. In cases where it was essential that an errand be done, she did it herself. If the errand was important but she could not do it, she gave specific directions and two reminders. Jack did not like this but she explained that it was for her own benefit. She used an "I feel" statement. "Jack, I feel less anxious if I give you two reminders." In this way she took responsibility for her feelings, shared her feelings with Jack, and took action. She chose a limit (*two* reminders) to avoid nagging. After two reminders she knew she had done all she could.

Linda and Jack's problem illustrates the third part of your plan to maintain constructive communication: selected assertive communication. Linda found that in following her plan she was inevitably confronted with this troubling defect in Jack. Yet, she brought up the subject of his failure to follow through only when necessary. She carefully prepared her wording so that she owned her responsibility and her side of the problem. And she assertively asked (not demanded) that Jack work on his part of the problem.

She would say, "This errand is important. So that I am less anxious about it I'm going to explain exactly what must be done and I'll give you a couple of reminders. I feel that is my part."

If Jack objected and said, "Oh, no. You really don't have to . . ." or picked a fight by saying, "You really don't trust me. You're treating me like a child," Linda would stay assertive but not become aggressive.

"I want to explain and give two reminders just for my own anxiety's sake. It will make me feel that I have done my part."

If Jack did not follow through—which was often the case— Linda did not "rub it in." Neither did she pretend she wasn't upset. She simply let Jack know she ended up doing it herself, and in order to maintain her serenity she forgave him.

After you have formed your plan, regular spot inventories and re-evaluations of your plan are advisable. You know your marriage problems, your character defects, and your spouse's character defects. You know how long it has taken to form these defects. Progress in resolving these issues will also take time. The willingness to stop and revise your plan will ensure the problems do get solved. If you have slipped back into acting out your character defect in retaliation for your spouse's hurtful actions, acknowledge it and stop. If you find yourself thinking in negative, self-defeating, and conflict-producing ways, ask your Higher Power's help to catch yourself in it and stop. Be open to the advice and support of others in Twelve Step programs. Seek individual counseling if you think it may be helpful. Although it takes time, real and long-lasting progress is possible—even inevitable—if you and your spouse continue to work the program. Even if your partner does not work a program you will see more clearly whether it is best for you to stay or leave if you have followed your personal plan.

<u>GREG AND JULIE</u>

Working their own programs, Greg and Julie managed to work through a crisis point. Greg grew in his awareness of how his character defects of insensitivity and self-centeredness hurt Julie. He made amends by practicing active listening. Julie realized her defect of character of verbally degrading and criticizing Greg in front of his friends had perpetuated their marriage problems. She made amends to Greg by esteeming him and refraining from criticizing him in front of their church friends.

Bitterness still remained.

"After all the progress we've made," Greg thought, "we still are not making love very often at all."

Greg and Julie had problems with their sex life. When the marriage problems were at their worst, they hardly ever made love. It was a source of continued resentment for them both.

"Julie has done a good job of controlling her sharp tongue when we're in a group. She doesn't seem to want sex as much as I do, though. I can't help thinking she must be holding something more against me. She says she has forgiven me, but then she'll criticize me when we discuss it. I'm not romantic enough. I don't dress attractively enough. I come on too strong. I demand sex. I sulk if I don't get it. She feels pressured by me."

Greg resolved to use the tools of his program to address this issue. He went all the way back to Steps One, Two, and Three. He named Julie's character defect.

"At this point, I'm dealing with Julie's tendency to criticize and blame me for the problem and to not take any responsibility for developing her sexuality and having some sense of romance."

Once he identified Julie's character defect, he released responsibility for it to God and to Julie. Using the Serenity Prayer, he resolved to accept and love Julie even with her character defects. Greg reviewed the first three steps in his journal. "This is the one area where I find it toughest to admit my powerlessness. There's got to be something I can do to make Julie respond."

Whenever Julie rejected Greg's romantic overtures he remembered every time she rejected him in the past. And he felt the same anger and hurt. He got in touch with yet another untapped reservoir of thoughts which fueled his anger and hurt.

"We'll never solve this problem."

"Julie is so stubborn."

"Julie has never been as aware of her sexuality as I am—and she never will be."

"There's something wrong with me. I'm just not doing the right things to satisfy her."

As Greg consciously forgave Julie for each incident of rejection in the past, he found he could more easily respond to his irrational thoughts about Julie and their sex life. He was, therefore, able to make progress releasing his present anger and hurt.

"We can solve this problem."

"Julie can be headstrong, but I will not label her stubborn all the time. She can also listen and understand what I'm saying."

"Julie's family was repressive and uptight about sex. But she has been responsive to me in the past and I know she can be again."

"There's nothing wrong with me. I will continue to work on myself in the areas I know I need to improve. I can be more attentive and sensitive. I can set up romantic situations—without pressuring her. I can dress better. And I know the problem is not all my fault or all my responsibility."

As Greg took this spot inventory using his Step Four material as a guide, he realized he had amends to make. The next time the subject of sex and romantic time came up Greg fully admitted his responsibility in the matter instead of blaming or pressuring Julie to change.

He said, "I know I haven't been as available as I could be because I have been working late. I know I could put more effort into planning romantic time. I could also pay more attention to the way I dress."

The hardest part for Greg was to resist the temptation to press Julie for similar admissions. He had to bite his tongue to prevent himself from pointing out how Julie's criticism, past rejection, and sometimes distant attitude had contributed to the problem.

Greg decided to closely examine the nature of his anger at Julie and the hurt feelings that lay beneath. Greg realized that the intensity of his anger with Julie was rooted in feelings of rejection. When Greg asked himself if he had ever experienced feelings of rejection of the same type before, he realized that many times he had.

Greg identified what he really wanted from Julie: unconditional acceptance. He traced his unfulfilled need for acceptance back to hurtful memories from his adolescence and his childhood. His current conflict with Julie was in some ways rooted in conflicts of the past. For example, Greg remembered being teased for not dressing in style as a teenager. Julie teased him about that. Greg also remembered the depth of his hurt feelings as a teen.

"My parents never let me buy the clothes I wanted. Sometimes they forced me to wear certain clothes. I knew I'd be made fun of by the other kids but I had to wear those clothes or my parents would yell at me."

Greg remembered that his awkwardness around girls as a teenager was associated with feeling rejected, left out, and angry at his mother for making him wear "stupid, nerdy" clothes. Some of his feelings about his mother and girls in general at that time in his life unconsciously fueled his conflict with Julie today.

Julie worked on the problem from her side. She had forgiven Greg's insensitivity in the past. She found it difficult to forgive him for his current behavior of working late, forgetting to call, and then coming home and slumping onto the couch.

Julie felt like giving up. "Greg can't be pleased. Even if we have a great time sexually, he isn't satisfied. He just wants more. I end up feeling pressured."

Julie saw Greg's character defect as insensitivity and a tendency to try to control her. She admitted her powerlessness over Greg and his faults. But releasing Greg's character defect to God and Greg seemed like giving up hope to her. "I can forgive the past, but I don't want to go on and on."

When Greg made an effort to do something sweet and romantic Julie's heart would melt just as quickly as her resentment had risen. At those times she could see that Greg was making some effort to fulfill her wants and needs. She found willingness within herself to creatively try to improve the situation. She would put a lot of energy into planning time together, but she would feel disappointed if Greg didn't respond the way she thought he should.

Julie implemented Step Ten in a different way than Greg. She did not write very much in her journal, but found it more helpful to think over her relationship with Greg and write down a few notes to herself in her journal later. She felt she had forgiven the past, but when a fresh incident occurred, she felt all the anger and hurt rush back. At those times she became aware of the thoughts which formed the root of her anger and hurt.

"Greg will never be the kind of man I've always wanted him to be."

"He blames me for our sexual problems."

"He's always going to be a poor dresser. Hell will freeze over before he pays any attention to his appearance!"

At first, Julie found it hard to take a spot inventory and to figure out her part in the problem. She went back over her Step Four Inventory and realized that one thing she could immediately work on was her tendency to lash back at Greg. She reviewed her decision to use assertiveness rather than "sharp-tongued criticism."

Promptly admitting responsibility for Julie took the form of an apology to Greg for her sharp comments as soon as she could do it sincerely. Along with the apology, she said to Greg what she would have said if she had been assertive rather than aggressive. Also, she spent time thinking about what she wanted to say to Greg and how she could convey how she really felt in a way he could understand.

Julie's spot inventory consisted first of becoming aware of her irrational thoughts, rationally responding to each one, and finally formulating an apology for her "barbs" and an assertive statement of what she really meant to say.

Her reformulated thoughts went something like:

"It's not that Greg will never be more attractive and sensitive. He is trying, but his progress isn't as fast as I want it to be."
"He does tend to blame me. I want him to take his responsibility to improve himself instead of blaming me."
"He's making an effort to dress nicer."
"He's not doing a great job but I will apologize for my cutting comments about him and tell him what I think would look nice on him instead—and then let it go."

The progress Julie and Greg made concerning their sex life was slow because of the sensitive nature of the subject. They were both filled with a lot of hurt and resentment. Their successful efforts encouraged them even if things were not yet perfect. By each working his or her own program they were able to persevere.

STEP GUIDE: STEP TEN

Step Ten is continuing your personal inventory. The best way to continue your personal inventory is to take the opportunity when you feel hurt and angry at your partner to get back in touch with all of your Twelve Step work thus far.

1. When you feel angry or hurt by your partner go back to Step One. Name the character defect which is hurting you the most. Name your need which remains unfulfilled.

2. Admit your powerlessness over your partner and his or her character defect. You cannot resolve your partner's problem. You cannot force your partner to work on the problem. Release the responsibility for your partner's character defect to God and to your partner. Accept the current situation as it really is. Accept your partner as a lovable person even with his or her character defect. Remember that accepting your partner does not mean submitting to abuse of any type, but rather means respecting and loving your partner, faults and all.

3. Call to mind the incidents in the past when your partner has hurt you as a result of the same character defect. Search your memory for hurtful incidents in your childhood or adolescence when you felt any similar hurt or resentment. Seek to forgive those who hurt you. Become aware of the damaging and ongoing effects of these hurtful incidents. Allow your Higher Power to provide for your unfulfilled needs in the past. Allow a healing of these specific hurtful memories. Rationally respond to any irrational beliefs about yourself, God, or your partner which may be rooted in the hurts of the past. Remember, the intensity of your hurt and anger today is often linked to hurtful memories of the past.

4. Take inventory of your current behavior. Identify the ways in which you unintentionally cooperate with and enable the problem. Admit your character defect's role in the problem. Take responsibility for your part of the problem. Abstain from behaviors that make matters worse.

5. Admit your responsibility to your partner. Make verbal di-

rect amends for your part, however small. Ask forgiveness. Ask your partner for help in identifying your part of the responsibility for the problem.

6. Do the following exercise[2] to clearly identify the issues that require amends making in your relationship today.

A. Make a list of all the specific behaviors that currently fuel your resentment toward your partner. When do you feel most frustrated, angry, sad, hurt, and resentful? This is Julie's partial list:

I feel angry and hurt when you

- don't listen to me.

- ignore me when I'm hurt or crying.

- refuse to acknowledge my ideas for our business.

B. Next write what you want in each situation in clear and positive language. This is Julie's list:

- I want to feel understood by you.

- I'd like you to comfort me when I'm crying.

- I want you to listen to my ideas.

- I would like you to spend time with me.

C. Finally form a specific request that corresponds to each item on your list. Each request should be clear and positive and describe a specific behavior. This is Julie's list (note that these requests are positive and specific):

- I would like you to listen to my feelings for just ten minutes when you first come home from work.

- When I'm upset I want you to hug me and listen to my feelings.

• When I tell you an idea, I want you to spend five or ten minutes telling me if you like it or not and why.

• When I ask for your attention, I want you to drop what you are doing and talk to me or tell me when we can talk.

D. Ask your partner to make his or her three lists. Exchange the last two lists (what you want and behavior requests). Use your communication skills (see Chapter Nine) to clarify your specific requests. If your partner won't cooperate with this exercise, make your best guess at what he or she would say.

E. Rank the importance of each of your requests on a scale of 1–100. 1 is not important. 100 is extremely important.

F. Rank your partner's requests in terms of difficulty. 1 is not difficult. 100 is very difficult.

G. Use your partner's list as a guide for ongoing amends making and spot inventory. Make a commitment to yourself to give your partner at least two or three items on his or her list each week. Remember that these changes are part of your ongoing program. They are gifts not bargaining chips.

You may repeat this exercise with your partner as often as you find it is helpful.

CONTINUE YOUR PERSONAL INVENTORY

1.

FOCUS ON YOUR PARTNER'S CHARACTER DEFECT

Which character defect is hurting you the most?

2.

RELEASE IT TO GOD AND YOUR PARTNER

*Admit your powerlessness.
*Release responsibility for character defect to God and your partner.
*Accept your partner, character defect and all.

3.

ALLOW HEALING OF MEMORIES

*What is your unfulfilled need?
*Remember past incidents which involve this character defect of your partner.
*Forgive past and present incidents.
*Become aware of your thoughts and feelings rooted in the past.
*Rationally respond to your irrational thoughts.

4.

TAKE INVENTORY

*What is your part in the problem?
*Which of your character defects is operative?
*Take 100% responsibility.

5.

PROMPTLY ADMIT YOUR RESPONSIBILITY

*Make a verbal, direct amends; ask forgiveness for your part of the problem.

6.

MAKE A PLAN AND IMPLEMENT IT

*What can you do to improve on your character defect?
*What communication skills are important to improve in yourself to address the problem?
*How can you make it easier for your partner to take responsibility?
*How can you assertively ask your partner for what you want?

7.

ONGOING RE-EVALUATION

*Think over the current status of your plan. Can you improve it? How?
*Have you slipped back into overt acting out of your character defect?
*Practice assertive forgiveness, cf. Chapter 11.

CONTACT

> **STEP ELEVEN: WE SOUGHT THROUGH PRAYER AND MEDITATION TO IMPROVE OUR CONSCIOUS CONTACT WITH GOD, AS WE UNDERSTOOD HIM, PRAYING ONLY FOR THE KNOWLEDGE OF HIS WILL AND THE POWER TO CARRY THAT OUT.**

In every loving relationship there is an ever-present desire to be in the other person's thoughts. Lockets and rings are given to remind the lovers of what they share, drawing them together at least mentally if not physically. Hearing the other person's voice or receiving a letter puts them in contact. This same desire for contact is behind prayer. "It seems the meaning of prayer lies in man's aspiration to be thought of by God as one who is thinking of Him."[1] A prayer, therefore, is a word or gesture that places you in closer contact with God.

The awkwardness of gestures, touch, and language frustrates the desire for contact by their inadequacy. Words fail to capture the intensity of feeling or meaning of an experience. Yet, we go on trying to express love and forgiveness because, despite the ineffability of love, the words give us access to the power or energy generated by the relationship. As overused as the word *love* is, it still feels good to say it and to hear it. It connotes a reality that is ever new.

A prayer is defined by its *intent* rather than *content*. It may take verbal form, such as a poetic verse or sacred text, or a nonverbal form, as in evocative images or reflective thinking. Prayer may also take bodily form by the use of certain postures, kneeling for example. The intention of prayer, here, is to deepen your contact with God and to direct you in the knowledge of his will with respect to your own character defects; to help you surrender your life and marriage over to God; and to arrest the distorted thinking that makes your life and marriage unhappy.

CONSCIOUS CONTACT

Your Twelve Step work makes you conscious of your own needs and desires. You have learned how mental habits are formed to get those needs and desires satisfied. Some strategies are helpful and effective, others are not. In unraveling the beliefs behind the emotions, you have no doubt experienced how difficult it is to keep those bad mental habits from reasserting themselves. Any progress to counteract this tendency has come from maintaining a complete reliance on your Higher Power. Gratitude for this progress forms the central experience of prayer.

In the experience of gratitude you become aware of some benefit, some advancement that was not entirely of your own making. This is the spiritual awakening which dawned when you became aware of a power greater than yourself that has the power to restore your life and marriage to wholeness. The words which form your prayers or inspire your thoughts endeavor to say thank you. Thankfulness expressing gratitude invites continuation of that contact.

Prayer as an openness to God, then, is based on experience: restlessness, hunger, and yearning, as well as contentment, gratitude, or wonder. But it is an invitation, a reaching out to God who is present. This experience may give rise to certain images or thoughts, but like expressing love, they are at best analogous. They leave us wanting to say more. A prayer leaves us gazing toward a horizon, expecting a future.

Back in Chapter Three, Jerry and Therese were struggling with their marriage because both were searching for something more meaningful in their relationship. Jerry believed more frequent sexual contact would achieve this. Therese saw their sex life as something routine and sought other expressions of intimacy, such as long walks and conversation. In order to resolve their problems, they were forced inward: 1) to acknowledge the other's needs and desires; 2) to examine their own thoughts and intentions; 3) to restructure any controlling thoughts; 4) to seek an acceptable course of action through prayer and meditation; and 5) to pray for the strength to take the action. Working it out was a daily struggle, but daily they made it work.

On any given day Jerry or Therese might say that he or she was unhappy about something. However, the degree of dissatisfaction was the conclusion to an internal process of evaluation. "Why should I put up with this?" is a question answerable only from within oneself. The more at home you are with your own interior life, the more dedicated you are to improving your own judgment and contact with God, the greater ease you will have in resolving conflicts. No marriage is ever perfect—that is an irrational expectation. But even imperfect marriages can be happy ones—this is a reasonable expectation.

Through prayer and daily personal inventories Jerry and Therese tried to keep the focus on what they were doing to encourage each other to be open and trusting. This meant self-examination on a regular basis, such as taking an inventory; reviewing the details of events in an open, prayerful way; looking for half-truths, resentments, boasting, and so on. Any retreat into defensiveness or grandiosity was exposed and confessed as soon as possible.

Messy though it sometimes was at first, the homework they did internally made communicating sensitive issues easier. When they prayed about something and sought to know what God's will was and how to carry it out, they felt a greater security about putting everything out on the table. Similarly, the issues that persisted between them reflected their internal struggles as individuals more than misdeeds done against one another.

Step Eleven helped Jerry in his work with his temper. In trying to discover the origins of this defect, he searched through his past but was unable to make any headway. He could not find any thread that really helped him explain why he was the way he was. Yet, it was a persistent problem he wanted to do something about. He began to feel frustrated and self-conscious.

Eventually he came to a working conclusion. He decided that, for some reason, he was not able to trace the origins of this defect. Nevertheless, it was there. Rather than straining over it, he acknowledged he was powerless over this area of his personality. He turned it over to God, admitting it was a problem and that he had very little insight into solving the problem. Just the same, he resolved to work on it as it occurred in the present. Rather than looking back into his childhood, he would simply look to the last flare-up and deal with that. He would take responsibility and make amends as soon as possible. By working with each incident while it was fresh, he gained perspective on how this defect was presently working its way into his life and marriage. In his meditation he examined the things that triggered his temper and considered better ways of expressing his emotions. He prayed daily for guidance and strength to overcome this character defect.

PRAYER

There are many wonderful books and guides to prayer. The advice of others can be helpful, but there is no wrong way to pray. The main thing is to pray the way *you* pray. The best aids for prayer will emphasize your own individuality and creative powers of choice. They will be simple and straightforward. Avoid what appears to ascribe to rigid principles or vague anecdotes. Life is not as simple as it seems, so resist anything that makes it sound too easy. Don't be afraid to be critical. Your best asset is your own common sense.

Regular discipline at prayer works best. Before you begin something, offer a prayer of surrender. When you have completed something, offer a prayer of thanksgiving, no matter how things turn out. A steady diet of prayer and meditation keeps a check on the influence of your own controlling mind, which continually seeks to reassert itself.

One method of prayer is described below. It shifts your focus from you to God. Particularly in conflict, seeing beyond your own fears and insecurities is difficult. Your ego defenses distort your perspective. Prayer tries to get you out of the way in order to illuminate your mind and heart with as much of God as possible.

Prayer leads to a natural kind of meditation or reflection and vice versa. Insights arise when you are able to clear away your initial point of view. Prayer is an openness to God speaking to the events of your life, more than it is God listening to what you have to say. Often the concern you have over a particular issue rivets your attention to one or two interpretations, usually with negative overtones. Prayer implies a release. You allow the facts to fly up like open hands and let the outcome fall where it may. You release the problem by putting it in God's hands. This permits your mind to relax enough to imagine a new solution. To see what you do not now see is the object of each meditation. Prayer is openness to God breaking through to reveal the possibility of a new interpretation or to confirm your present response.

CENTERING PRAYER

Centering prayer is a very old method of prayer. It is practiced with many adaptations and in a variety of religions. It is compatible with any philosophy or religion you subscribe to. It is called centering prayer because it centers or focuses your attention on the presence of God within you, while heightening your ability to distinguish between what is you and what is not you, what are your thoughts and what comes from God. Being centered in your true self helps you detach yourself from the emotions you are feeling and to experience relaxation, serenity, and hope.

Every object has a center of gravity, a point at which the object's weight is equally distributed. When the center is stable, the object is said to be in balance. While balanced the object can withstand great pressures against it. The extremities can change positions without disturbance. When the center is moved or upset, however, even the slightest pressure or push can send the thing tumbling over.

You have a center of gravity. If you stand on one foot you shift that center. So long as you maintain a balance you are all right. If that center gets pushed too far to one side, however, you are sent sprawling. There is also a psychological and spiritual center within you as well. This center is a state, not a place. It is where the various complexities that make up your personality and your particular situation at a given moment converge, creating in you a state of balance or equilibrium. In this state of equilibrium you can withstand the various pressures that act against you, while maintaining the integrity of your personality.

This center of gravity is a function of your true self. The true self pulls together the various powers within you, lining them up and making them work for you, rather than tumbling headlong into chaos. Your center is where the sum total of your physical, psychological, and spiritual powers come together.

Balance is always something to reach for. Thus, the spiritual life is characterized by a continuous striving or seeking new forms of harmony and integration. Each day's prayer and meditation strives to make more connections between the apparent contradictions and confusion in your life.

At certain moments of life you may emphasize the cerebral—to be thought oriented. You may find it necessary to carefully think over your next move and analyze the arguments in coming to a decision. At other times of your life you may be more viscerally inclined—tending toward your emotions and instincts. Christmas time, for example, is a time when sentiments run high. Adjusting to the ebb in flow of life is why a daily routine of prayer and meditation is imperative.

How do you know you have reached a balance? Temperaments are different, so it is hard to say, except through self-discovery. When you are sick, for example, it is hard to think clearly or be sensitive to the needs of others. No one ever achieves perfect balance. It is something you strive for daily by increasing your conscious contact with God.

Marriage conflict brings many forces to bear against you. Equilibrium takes more effort and more time to achieve. Allow yourself extra time to re-establish balance. Your marriage is the most important human relationship you have. It only stands to reason that it will present the most important challenges to you.

Serenity is something worked out partly by what you do and partly by what you do not do. Like standing on one foot, balance is achieved both by exercising muscle control and by letting the forces of gravity work against you. Serenity and stability in relationships like marriage depend equally on what you do as much as what you don't do.

What you do, of course, is work your own program: take your own inventories, and take responsibility for your own defects of character. What you do not do is try to run your spouse's program: blame him or her for troubles, or try to analyze or make choices for him or her.

Centering prayer helps you reach the state of equilibrium. It is the center from which you relate to everyone else. It is not any particular emotion you are trying to evoke, though emotions do emerge quite spontaneously. The purpose of centering prayer is not to dwell on your own thoughts or emotions. Centering prayer opens you to encounter God. You may spend a considerable amount of time in prayer and have nothing to show for it in the way of changed attitudes or new ideas. If a friend invites you over to his or her house for dinner, you wouldn't admire the china and then take it home with you. Likewise, in prayer, you are in another's domain; look, admire, let it inspire you. There are times when what occurs to you while in prayer will be inexpressible to others. But remember, prayer is not going to enable you to further your own ends. You pray in order to know God's will for you and to receive the power to carry that out.

STARTING TO PRAY

Picture what you are about to do as though you were plunging into the depths of the ocean. You cannot just drop to the bottom. That would be too dangerous. There is a compression process you have to go through. While in prayer you will have experiences and insights that will seem very important to you. You will think these events are calling you to do something, which excites you and leads you to believe you are making progress. You may remain, for a time, at a given level or depth of prayer and feel very good, or you may feel very frustrated at how slow your progress is. In either case, at some point you will sense the need to go deeper, to abandon the images and concepts you have of God for something richer. Trust God and let go some more.

You will sense the way you pray has become, once again, an area in which you are in control. You will sense your prayer is full of lots of you and very little of God; you will wonder if you have ever prayed at all. You have not yet reached the bottom. You can still grow closer to God.

Your relationship with God is also a spiral in which risk and trust yield greater experiences of intimacy. Prayer parallels a conversation, requiring patience to listen and a willingness to take risks.

First, begin by putting yourself in a quiet place. Pick a place where you won't be disturbed. Turn off the radio or television. Sit in a comfortable position, or lie on the floor if you like.

Allow yourself fifteen or twenty minutes to pray. Close your eyes and open your mind and heart. Let God start the conversation. A word, a thought, or an image will come to mind, calling you to an awareness of God's presence. Because of the conflict you are currently living through, dust off the word or image that comes to mind by dismissing negative, defeatist impulses. In the process stray thoughts will pop very quickly into your head. Let them pass from your attention as quickly as they come. As in any conversation, you can be interrupted by many intrusions.

These intrusions may be from within you as well as around you. Because of the importance of the conversation, you are having to set these stray thoughts aside. You can come back to them later if they are truly important.

These distractions are promptings of your own energy. They cloud your awareness like steam on a mirror. You may have a good idea about something. You may begin to feel very peaceful or on the contrary you may feel very disturbed, sad, or lonely. Some emotions may scare you. Do not focus on any particular emotion. Let them pass. They are products of your own doing. They may be very good, but at this time you are more interested in what God has to say than what you have to say. Let your thoughts and emotions pass through you as freely as they come.

When you find yourself progressing to deeper, quieter states of being, you will begin to notice changes in your moods and thoughts. This is the result of your relaxing and shifting attention. Thoughts will occur to you that have not previously. Take notice of these changes, but let them go too. You want to plunge as deeply as you can into the oneness you have already with God. The more you focus on yourself the less aware of God you will be.

Centering prayer is a kind of motionless attention. It means that you fix your attention on God and not on yourself. It is hard because you are so full of your own concerns and future. Your desire to improve your conscious contact with God is like the hand of a captain at the helm of his ship, steering his boat through the dark night. He is guided by his instruments. He put his trust in them and not only in his own sight.

Centering prayer means to be attentive. You are not merely sleeping or drifting passively through dream states, although you may fall asleep and dream. (Sleep is not prayer, but it may be just as necessary, especially when you are under a great deal of stress. If this happens, enjoy it! See it as a gift. When you awaken, turn your attention back to prayer.)

Do not become discouraged when you are distracted or fall asleep. The more you focus on what you are doing the more you are focusing on you and not God. Return to the sacred word and refocus. Beginners worry whether they are praying correctly. If you are worrying about it, you aren't. Let go and try not to focus on you as much as on God in you.

The overall experience of prayer will yield little that you can tell others about. The purpose of prayer is not to produce any particular thing. Rather, it is to increase your conscious contact with your Higher Power, God as you understand the meaning of the term. Remember, God is of no use to you. That is, you cannot control Him. The aim of prayer is to seek His will for you.

Once you re-enter the work-a-day world you may sense a change in your disposition. You may feel you have more of a grasp on things; but not necessarily. You may never be able to say for sure that "God told me to do thus and so." This does not mean you have not prayed well or are doing anything wrong. The point of prayer is not what you produce, but to be with God.

As you persevere in prayer you will notice insights emerge. Deeply rooted fears and beliefs surface. As you let these float to consciousness your conscious attitudes will adapt because of them. You cannot search for these profound insights; you will have to wait for them to come to you. As they occur, consider them in light of what is taking place in your marriage. Trust God, and let these insights direct your actions.

FORGIVENESS AND PRAYER

As we have mentioned, forgiveness in the Twelve Steps means the cancellation of an emotional and spiritual debt. Forgiveness is not just a one-time decision, but an ongoing attitude. It is impossible to remain willing to make amends until a forgiving attitude has been adopted.

Forgiveness, like love, begins with a decision and moves on to affect your feelings. It starts in the mind and moves into your heart. You have already moved through part of the process by working a Twelve Step program. You forgave your spouse for past offenses. But what about present and future offenses? How can you stay willing to make amends for your offenses against your partner when you know you will be hurt again?

You have already seen the destructive effects control has on your marriage. Resentment and holding on to past hurts lock your own heart into a destructive cycle that serves no useful purpose. The willingness to keep on forgiving comes from your Higher Power. It requires only your faith to release control of your partner. Instead of practicing coercion or control to get your partner to change, you exercise honesty, faith, and forgiveness.

Without control what other power do you have to influence your spouse? Only God. You trust that God will work in your partner's heart and that your partner will respond to God's call. It may take time, but your partner can respond to God just as you have. The best way to support your partner is to continue work on correcting your own character defects and to make amends for past and current hurts. Your prayer is for knowledge of God's will for your marriage and the power to carry it out.

Maryln had come through so much with her husband, John, that if she sat down and thought about it long enough she began to cry. They started out as most couples do, with hardly anything. Maryln remembered the early days and all the fun times they shared. She also remembered the hard times when she did her Step Four Inventory and her Step Six healing of memories work.

As long as they had been together, John had had trouble controlling his temper. At times it was so bad Maryln didn't think she could take any more. John could be so mean and verbally abusive she questioned whether he really loved her.

"How can he love me," she thought, "and still curse at me and put me down in such a vicious way?"

While their son, Chris, was growing up he was the target of John's temper. Maryln was deeply resentful of this. Most of her arguments with John concerned their son. Maryln disagreed with John's authoritarian parenting style. She was disgusted by the way he issued orders and expected Chris to obey them with no discussion. She allied herself with Chris and defended him when he was a victim of John's verbal abuse.

This pattern had gone on for years, when John's career as a military officer caused an involuntary separation. He was assigned to a duty station where the family could not go. Maryln was relieved and secretly glad that it happened. During the long separation she had an affair with a male friend who offered her emotional support. She knew that this relationship could not develop long term because she still loved John, in spite of his faults. They were reunited after John was transferred again. Maryln was surprised that John did not go into a rage when he found out about the affair. Instead, he was silent about the matter and seemed hurt.

As Maryln and John's marriage problems progressed, Chris's problems emerged. Although he was quite intelligent, he routinely brought home Ds and Fs. He refused to accept responsibilities around the house. As a teenager, he became more and more out of control. He disregarded basic house rules. Maryln repeatedly caught him in lies about his homework, chores, and his whereabouts. Whenever he was granted a privilege like using the car he seemed to repay Maryln with an insult, lying about where he had been or leaving the car filthy or with an empty gas tank.

Maryln decided to work a Twelve Step program to rebuild her marriage. She recalled each hurtful experience while working her Step Four Inventory. She discovered that past hurts formed the basis of her character defects of unfaithfulness, emotional withdrawal, nagging, and controlling behavior.

As she completed Step Six and became ready to turn her character defects over to God, Maryln asked God to heal the hurts she suffered at the hands of her family. She forgave each incident in her heart as best she could.

When it came time to take Step Eight it almost seemed to Maryln that she would have to start over from scratch.

"I'm supposed to do what?" she protested. "Become willing to make amends? What if I'm not willing? What if I'm fed up?"

Maryln was fed up. She had had it with John's temper and Chris's dishonesty and irresponsibility. She wanted to give up. She questioned her Twelve Step commitment.

"What would 'giving up' mean? Leaving? No. I've decided to stay. There's no running away from it."

Maryln knew from her previous Twelve Step work that she had character defects which hurt her husband and son, as well as herself. Before she could become willing to make amends to others she had to make amends to herself by taking assertive action.

She released past hurts she had suffered by reviewing her Step Six entries in her journal. With Chris, this meant recalling the most hurtful examples of times when he had betrayed her trust, lied to her, and shown grossly irresponsible behavior. With John, it meant recalling the worst examples of his verbal abuse. She forgave Chris and John all over again.

She made a decision to prevent more damage in her relationships with Chris and John by practicing detachment with love in all her dealings with them. She applied the One Hundred Percent Responsibility Rule, taking all of her responsibility and none of theirs. She prayed for the strength and guidance to do this well. The most helpful prayer for this purpose was the Serenity Prayer.

In actually applying one hundred percent responsibility, Maryln found it necessary to stop doing the things she knew were contributing to the chaos. With Chris, this meant she would not lecture him the next time he lied to her. She would stop nagging him to do his homework and chores. She would stop yelling. She knew threats didn't work, especially when she had no intention of carrying them out. With John, she tried to stop doing the things she knew he perceived as controlling. She hated his temper, but she decided that venting her anger about his anger had become counterproductive.

She knew what was not helping, but she didn't really know what would help. In making a decision to assertively stop submitting to Chris's and John's offensive behavior she had to think creatively about what to do when they "started up" again. Chris lied almost every day about one thing or another. She decided that the most assertive thing to do would be to stop believing him. She stopped listening to what she believed were lies, even if sometimes they were not. She simply couldn't tell the difference anymore. She required Chris to verify his word even though he complained loudly.

ASSERTIVE FORGIVENESS

1.

IDENTIFY EACH PERSON WHOM YOU HURT

For Maryln: Her son, Chris, and her husband, John.

2.

RERELEASE PAST HURTS YOU HAVE SUFFERED

For Maryln: With Chris Maryln recalled examples of his lying, betrayal, irresponsibility and forgave each offense using Step Six worksheet. With John, Maryln recalled examples of his angry outbursts at herself and the kids, and examples of him holding grudges for days or weeks. She forgave each offense using the Step Six process.

3.

MAKE A DECISION TO PREVENT FURTHER DAMAGE TO YOUR RELATIONSHIP AS BEST YOU CAN

For Maryln: She decided to apply the 100% Responsibility Rule in her relationships with Chris and John. She used the Serenity Prayer each day to order her thoughts about Chris and John.

4.

STOP ABUSIVE AND OFFENSIVE BEHAVIORS

For Maryln: She identified what she did to make the problem worse and decided to abstain. With Chris, she knew nagging him did not help. She knew threatening him with punishments she did not intend to follow through with did not help. With John, she recognized her controlling behavior and attitude toward his temper. She knew nagging him did not help. She knew smoldering inside and staying angry for days at him was not helping.

5.

> ASSERTIVELY STOP SUBMITTING TO ABUSIVE AND OFFENSIVE BEHAVIOR
>
> For Maryln: When Chris lied to her and she suspected it, she decided to end the conversation. She stopped giving him trust where he had not earned it. She required verification of Chris's word without apology. When John blew up, she left the room saying she would return in 10 minutes when he had calmed down. Without holding a grudge herself, she would ask John to forgive what he had found offensive in her behavior. If he would not or if they disagreed on what happened Maryln forgave him in her heart and resolved to bring it up again when it naturally came up.

6.

> CONCENTRATE YOUR ENERGY ON HEALING YOUR PARTNER. USE THE EXERCISE DESCRIBED IN THE STEP TEN STEP GUIDE.
>
> For Maryln: She asked John to make a list of her hurtful behaviors, what he wanted, and specific behavior requests. She consistently gifted him with two or three specific behaviors a week.

Finally, as part of her Step Eleven, Maryln took it all to God in prayer. She prayed for the strength to fully forgive John and Chris for all offenses past, present, and future. She prayed for the clarity of thought to understand more and more her part of the problems between them. She prayed through her decisions to take assertive action and asked her Higher Power if her actions had been truly assertive or self-willed that day. She did her best, day by day, to stop enabling John and Chris by subtly cooperating with their disrespectful behavior toward her. If she did not like something they said or did, she said so, without nagging or complaining.

Finally, Maryln decided to concentrate her energy on healing her relationship. She consistently gifted John with two or three of the specific behaviors he wanted from her every week. The most difficult for Maryln was John's request that she tell him immediately in a positive way when something upset her. She could easily stop complaining, but it was hard for her to express her anger directly yet respectfully, especially when John did not do so. But she knew her work to be ongoing and that she would not give up on herself, her husband, or her son.

STEP GUIDE: STEP ELEVEN

Use this simple format to guide your meditation and prayer:

1. Using your journal, recall the events of the day. If you are praying in the morning, consider what lies ahead for you. If you are praying in the evening, consider the events that have just occurred.

2. Name the five most inspiring moments of the day. Name the five more trying moments. Recall them with all honesty and humility.

3. Identify any areas of need, any character defects that play a part, any amends you need to make to someone.

4. Affirm your need for God's help in your marriage.

5. Spend ten to fifteen minutes in Centering prayer.

6. Offer a personal prayer of thanks for the blessings received. The following is given as an example:

Today, God, You have blessed me and challenged me. I know in all things You love me. I am not always strong or know what is Your will, but I want to do what is right and good. I also know You never give us more than we can handle. Help me to accept the life You have given me this day, for I know that it is Your gift to me. Amen.

Some additional thoughts on prayer:

- Establish a set pattern of prayer, that is, a specific time each day, a specific place. This helps build support for a healthy habit.

- Ask God to direct your prayer. Ask His help to keep you from self-pity and self-seeking thoughts.

- Ask God for guidance in reaching decisions.

- Ask God's help in specific matters regarding your marriage and your willingness to love your spouse.

- Pray to be delivered from your own will. Prayer is a means of putting yourself in God's hands.

- Ask God for help for others, not just yourself.

- Throughout the day pause to pray and ask for God's help in all your affairs with others.

7. Complete the following Assertive Forgiveness Exercise in your journal. Remember to prayerfully ask your Higher Power for the knowledge of His will and the power to carry that out. Make your decisions about what assertive actions to take in the humble spirit of Step Eleven.

ASSERTIVE FORGIVENESS EXERCISE

1. **Identify each person whom you have hurt.**

2. **Rerelease past hurts you have suffered.** Use your Step 6 worksheets as a guide.

3. **Make a decision to prevent further damage to your relationship as best you can.** Apply the 100 Percent Responsibility Rule and The Serenity Prayer to order your thoughts.

4. **Stop your abusive and offensive behaviors.** Identify your specific behaviors that your partner considers abusive and offensive.

5. **Assertively stop submitting to abusive and offensive behavior.** Form a plan for responding assertively to your partner's hurtful behaviors.

6. **Decide on two or three specific behavior changes you will make.** Suggest two or three changes to your partner you would like him/her to make. Use the exercise in the Step Ten step guide.

12

RECOVERY

STEP TWELVE: HAVING HAD A SPIRITUAL AWAK-
ENING AS THE RESULT OF THESE STEPS, WE
TRIED TO CARRY THIS MESSAGE TO THOSE IN
TROUBLED MARRIAGE RELATIONSHIPS, AND TO
PRACTICE THESE PRINCIPLES IN ALL OUR AF-
FAIRS.

Last but not least, Step Twelve is the final step out of the isolation obsessive and controlling behavior leads you into. The real
thrust of spiritual renewal is to be able to live in harmony and
serenity with everyone. You started recovery by dealing with
the central relationship of your life, between you and God. You
saw how distorted your view of life had become without this
spiritual perspective. Everything and everyone appeared as
though they were put on this earth to serve you. No wonder
your spouse felt unappreciated or mistreated. No wonder you
began to feel alone and unloved.

The direction of your life and marriage has become a spiral of
increasing intimacy, deepening levels of trust, and honesty in
communication. The spats or arguments that are part of everyday life reveal something about your true self, rather than conceal it in defensiveness. Your spouse is no longer an enemy to
fear but a partner you can deal with.

The step you are about to take does much for continuing this
rising spiral of intimacy. You will multiply the insights you have
into yourself through the experiences you have with other per-

sons. The stories you hear of their struggles will make you see your own journey in a clearer light. The renewal you experience in your own life naturally will spread beyond yourself and your marriage. Most of all, you will see your own marriage, having been tried and tested, is even more precious for the process.

HAVING HAD A SPIRITUAL AWAKENING

What does "recovery" in marriage look like? Is it just the fact that you are still married? Isn't it also what kind of marriage you have? How fulfilling is it to both partners? How nurturing is it to your children?

Measuring progress in a relationship is never easy. There is always more that could be done. Problems can always be handled better. Viewpoints could be expressed better, more lovingly and humbly. Expressions of love and affection seem to always be imperfect. Energy must be continuously poured into a marriage relationship. Like pedaling a bicycle, the farther you want to go, the more you have to pedal. You cannot coast for long. The work of making your marriage go is a combination of ideals and actions, what you believe in and how you put that into practice.

Throughout this book, we have urged you to focus your mind as well as your heart on both sides of the issue. Controlling behavior tries to paint things in black or white, either/or terms. Whether in viewing your own character defects or those of your spouse, surrender and release of these difficulties to God brings about a vision that makes it possible to see a compromise, to experience a reconciliation of differences. From any single angle, there is going to be a blind spot. Nobody can see the back of his or her own head without the help of a mirror. With the patience to listen and learn from others, you can understand a great deal more than you could on your own.

It has been said that the single greatest sign of God's activity is the coming together of opposites. In God, all things are made one. The diversity of peoples, their opposing points of view, specific interests and needs are held together by an underlying unity. The spiritual awakening referred to throughout this book is a serenity that lets this diversity be. "Live and let live" is the slogan.

The whole discussion of character weaknesses was to show how character defects conceal a character strength. When well directed, you recover lost energy. You discover a new life. Do you see now that character defect and character strength are actually linked by your own being? A spiritual awakening no longer sees differences as absolutes or obstacles.

This spiritual vision extends to your spouse as well. Any two people are going to be limited in their capacity to handle a specific problem. When the starting point of your life and marriage is to do God's will, rather than your own, then neither of you has to be right. Both can be right or both could be wrong! You never place yourselves in no-win situations.

Through a willingness to really listen to and understand your partner, even when you disagree on one level, your commitment to each other and respect for one another's opinion reflect a deeper unity. Criticism does not have to be disrespectful. Anger is not necessarily unkind or unloving. Your own individuality does not exclude commitment and intimacy with your marriage partner. The narrow focus of the controlling mind misses these points of contact revealed by a deepening spiritual vision.

Marriage, because it continues throughout a couple's life, endures many changes. The ability to fall back on a firm foundation as you go through these events is the reason your marriage needs to flow out of your relationship with God. Likewise, the fulfillment you experience in your marriage will deepen your spiritual insights.

YOU HAVE NEED OF ME

You could ask, "Who doesn't need to improve their marriage?" Every relationship has some area that needs work. The perfect marriage does not exist. This does not imply every marriage is a troubled one. However, it may surprise you to learn whose marriage really is in need of serious medicine. It could be your best friend, who surprises you one day by telling you she is leaving her husband. It could be your boss, whose moods have been erratic and intolerable. Your own parents or your adult children may be experiencing estrangement in their marriages.

The following profile may help you in selecting someone as a possibility for a Step Twelve visit. Although every marriage has room for improvement, a troubled marriage stands out by the degree of frustration and hopelessness. Everybody has problems, but troubled couples do not seem to be able to resolve even common problems, much less something like adultery. The partner of a troubled marriage is worn down, frustrated by the other partner's resistance and the inability to make progress.

People usually do not go around talking about their marriage problems. In fact, depending on the degree of denial, they may have elaborate ways of glossing over the facts. Do not be fooled by clever wit or a casual brush-off. Taking time to hear what a person is NOT saying, as well as what he or she is, can confirm some of your suspicions.

A person trying to control a serious crisis in his or her life will have sudden changes in mood. He or she will grow increasingly isolated from friends, make out-of-character comments with peculiar twists or barbs attached. People sometimes make jokes about matters they are really hurting over. Impulsive behaviors, like shopping sprees or eating binges, reflect an internal struggle going on.

When you encounter such a person, keep in mind your own recovery and how strong willed you were when you first began. This empathy will do much in guiding you through a Step Twelve visit. Step Twelve should not be done hastily. If you approach a person without forethought and humility, the person may accuse you of butting into his or her private affairs. Remember the process of acceptance you had to go through. Just because you are convinced a person has need of this program does not mean he or she is. Be patient; go slow.

The kind of person you want to approach is someone who appears to be at wits' end. They are about to hit bottom. They have tried everything and nothing has worked. They may have tried marriage counseling with no improvement. At this point the person may be ready to surrender and accept his or her own powerlessness over the situation. This is the time to introduce the idea of a power greater than themselves who can help. A person at this stage may be ready to do more than just talk about his or her problems. Ask if you can suggest something positive he or she can actually do.

Sometimes people are not yet ready to act. They want to let off steam by "crying on someone else's shoulder." Be careful not to feed into the other person's ego by engaging in conversation that does not lead to any positive action. You are not there to gossip about the person's spouse or build up his or her case against the spouse.

Initially, the person may not really know what the problem is. The more obsessed he or she is about the marriage, the greater the chances that he or she has distorted the issues. Just talking about it can help clear up some of the confusion and make him or her feel better. Don't expect to solve all the problems or get him or her involved in the Twelve Step program. If you find it helpful, take along a copy of this book for the person to read. Point out the Marital Needs Inventory in Chapter One. That can get him or her started on identifying the core problems.

"Who am I to speak?" you may be asking yourself. Who better? A Step Twelve visit is an exercise in compassion. Your greatest resource is the experience you have had in your own marriage. This is the core of your message that you carry. You are not a marriage counselor but a friend. What works for another couple is up to them. You share what has worked for you. There is no single cause for marriage problems. You do not want to make it sound as though there are any simple solutions. Share what God has done in your marriage. Ask the person to explore the possibility that these Twelve Steps could also help in his or her own marriage.

It is a spiritual program. The person needs to trust in his or her Higher Power. Analyzing one's partner involves "getting into the head" where the will to control can take over. Share how your life changed when you finally understood what *powerlessness* and *surrender to a Higher Power* meant for you and your marriage.

Everything you say can and will be used against you. Some people will say you are taking sides. Others will complain because you are not. This is the way the controlling mind works. Don't be deterred. You are not coming as a savior, but as a friend. You are not looking for the person to develop a codependent relationship with you. You do not know all the answers. Just give them an honest description of the fellowship. The person is not making a commitment to you. You are there only because you want to help others in troubled marriages. If the individual does not want to listen, do not waste your time.

Meet the person alone, not with his or her partner. Don't be put in the place of defending one or the other's complaint. Don't become the referee in a family dispute. Pick a time when the person is likely to be most receptive to your message. Base your approach on the mood or personality of the other person. Anticipate resistance, anger, denial, and so on. Do not contradict the other person. Instead empathize, saying how you were like that too before you started the program. Commit to listening to the other's story. Offer to return for another visit if that seems helpful. Give the person time to think about it. If there is a second visit, invite them to a meeting then.

Give freely what has been given freely to you.

I HAVE NEED OF YOU

Putting yourself at the disposal of others is the greatest way to maintain your own program of recovery. After your initial recovery your life and marriage will change. There will be new issues and new problems to be solved. Each new stage of marriage brings with it new pressures. Your Twelve Step work will keep controlling tendencies in check. A person who does not keep that balance between concern for others and concern for self will slip back into a self-centered lifestyle. Step Twelve keeps you coming out of yourself. Help yourself by helping others.

Step Twelve work also includes attending fellowship meetings. Some people do not like attending meetings. They are shy about sharing personal matters with others. But maintain a practice of attending meetings just for that reason, to keep your own will from dictating what is and is not good for you. There is a collective wisdom that is shared. You can always learn something else. More importantly, you may have something to share that helps another person find hope for his or her own struggle. The climate of a common goal to renew and heal marriage will encourage you to make and keep goals on a continuing basis. If you are having a problem in your own life, listening to others can help you find a right perspective. Healing takes time. Merely staying together does not a marriage make, but it is a start. Step Twelve deepens insights for your own program.

Each relationship within the family will be altered by the improvement of marriage. Every relationship will have to be addressed in the same way as that with your spouse. The principles of acceptance, surrender to God, and amends making will need to be applied. The final part of Step Twelve is practicing these principles in all your relationships. This not only improves the quality of your relationships directly, but what works for one may work with another. Insight tends to foster more insight.

THE ACTIONS OF LOVE

Practicing the principles in all your affairs means doing the actions of love first and letting the fruits of those actions carry the day. Sometimes your own doubts and moods call into question the strategies you plan to improve your life. You are not sure whether what you are doing is right. What's the use? Sometimes you don't understand why you have to make amends. Do the actions of love first and the feelings will follow.

What are the actions of love? Learn by doing. Pray for your

spouse by name. Maintain a practice of daily inventories regarding your most troublesome character defects. Make amends to any and all you offend as quickly as possible. Especially with your spouse and family, work for better and deeper communication. Forgiveness of grave offenses requires vigilance so that resentment does not re-emerge. Monitor this in yourself. Give every issue over to God. Give thanks. Be grateful.

The diamond on your wedding band is made from an old lump of coal, submitted to a great deal of pressure for a very long time. Eventually, the pressure causes a transformation to take place. The coal becomes a hard, radiant diamond. This is an apt description for marriage and for the ongoing effort to practice these principles in all your relationships. The discipline is a pressure. Some days will be excruciating. Yet, in time, your own awareness will change, your ability to express and give yourself to your spouse will convince you that the relationship is in fact growing stronger and stronger. The strength of your marriage will reinforce each of your lives.

STEP GUIDE: STEP TWELVE

DOS AND DON'TS OF A STEP TWELVE CALL

- If the person does not want help, *do not* waste time. You could be helping someone else who does want to improve his or her marriage.

- See the person alone, if possible. *Do not* become the referee in a family dispute.

- Stick with your own experience. *Do not* debate about what is wrong with the person's spouse. It is not a matter of winning or losing, but doing what is right. Stress individual responsibility.

- *Do not* show intolerance or hatred toward marriage or divorce.

- Emphasize the spiritual nature of the program. *Do not* forget to explain God as a Higher Power, as understood by the individual.

There may be some reluctance to accept the idea of a Higher Power.

- If the person is interested in knowing how you worked through your marriage problems, *do* take the time and tell him or her exactly what happened to you.

- Outline the program as a program of action. *Do* show how through self-awareness you were able to straighten out your past and are now sharing your story to reinforce the benefits of your action for yourself.

- Offer the person friendship and companionship. *Do* what you can to help, but remember you are carrying the message and not the person.

- *Do* assure the person that he or she can achieve serenity in his or her marriage through a reliance on God and working to eliminate the effects of character defects.

- Set a time limit in your own mind. *Do* give the person time to think about what you have said. Offer to come again, if it would be helpful.

In making Step Twelve, your own experience will be your greatest resource. Before approaching someone, consider how these steps will benefit them. Answer the following questions to decide how and when to approach them:

- What is the person's name?

- Why do you think he or she needs this program?

- What are you willing to do for this person?

- What exactly will you say?

- Think about what your marriage was like before you entered the program.

- How did you come to the decision to turn your life over to the care of God?

- What happened once you began practicing these principles in your life?

- How do you feel today about yourself, God, and your marriage?

Perhaps you do not know anyone who is having such serious problems. How do you make Step Twelve then? At a Troubled Couples Anonymous meeting, give your name to the group leader and offer to help should someone need you. Share willingly at a TCA meeting of your experience. If you have a talent in public speaking, volunteer to make a presentation to a group in your church or community. Share the kinds of experiences you have had and how the principles employed in the program helped you.

Notes

Chapter 1.

1. *Sexaholics Anonymous* (Simi Valley: Sexaholics Literature, 1989), p. 45.

2. *Alcoholics Anonymous* (New York: 3rd edition, Alcoholics Anonymous, Inc., 1976), p. 66.

3. Aaron T. Beck, M.D., *Love Is Never Enough* (New York: Harper & Row, 1988), p. 47.

4. Adapted from W. R. Rucker, *Values and Human Behavior* (San Diego: Technological Applications Project, 1978).

Chapter 3.

1. *Alcoholics Anonymous.*

2. Adapted from *Alcoholics Anonymous*, p. 63.

Chapter 4.

1. Harville Hendrix, *Getting the Love You Want: A Guide for Couples* (New York: Henry Holt, 1988).

2. Beck, p. 38.

Chapter 5.

1. Charles H. Browning, Ph.D., and Beverly J. Browning, Ph.D., *Private Practice Handbook* (Los Alamitos: Duncliff's International, 1986), p. 151.

2. Taken from William Shipley's philosophy class lectures, University of San Diego, CA, 1977.

Chapter 6.

1. John Bradshaw, *Homecoming: Reclaiming and Championing Your Inner Children* (New York: Bantam Books, 1990).

Chapter 8.

1. Beck, in *Love Is Never Enough,* chapter 7, gives eleven examples of typical distortions couples experience. These are an adaptation.

Chapter 9.

1. George Bach and Peter Wyden, *The Intimate Enemy: How to Fight Fair in Love and Marriage* (New York: Avon Books, 1968).

Chapter 10.

1. Bach and Wyden.

2. Adapted from Hendrix, p. 224.

Chapter 11.

1. Abraham J. Heschel, *Quest for God: Studies in Prayer and Symbolism* (New York: Crossroads Publishing, 1982), p. 10.

Appendix

Troubled Couples Anonymous is a fellowship of individuals whose primary goal is helping persons improve the quality of their marital relationships. The only requirement for membership is the desire to overcome obstacles to intimacy. There are no dues or fees.

For information send a self-addressed stamped envelope to:

Troubled Couples Anonymous
P.O. Box 600370
San Diego, CA 92160-0370

The Center for Relationship Recovery is an organization founded by the authors to provide professional assistance, marriage counseling, education, seminars, and training based on the principles outlined in this book.

For information call:

1-800/25-RENEW
(1-800/257-3639)

If the number is not operative from your area, send a self-addressed stamped envelope to:

The Center for Relationship Recovery
3638 Camino del Rio, North, Suite 200
San Diego, Ca 92108

About the Authors

Mark J. Luciano, Ph.D., is a licensed clinical psychologist and a licensed marriage and family therapist. In his private practice he has counseled hundreds of individuals and couples, helping them to work through their problems and revitalize their marriages. He has done research into the effects of alcoholism on marriage and family life, written articles for newspapers and magazines, and is a frequent public speaker and workshop leader.

He lives in San Diego, California, with his wife, Shelley, and their two children, Claire and Alexander.

The Reverend Christopher Merris holds a Master in Theology from the University of Louvain, Belgium, and is currently studying Family Therapy at the University of San Diego. He is a Catholic priest in parish ministry and is a Chaplain for the divorced and separated for the San Diego Diocese. He has worked extensively with troubled marriages and the divorced and is cofounder with Dr. Luciano of Troubled Couples Anonymous. He has been a guest lecturer at San Diego State University and the University of San Diego and is a frequent public speaker and workshop leader, conducting retreats and workshops for the divorced and separated.

He lives in San Diego, California.